Sent into the Lord's Vineyard

Sent into the Lord's Vineyard

Explorations in the Jesuit Constitutions

Brian O'Leary SJ

© *The Way*
First published 2012 by
Way Books, Campion Hall,
Oxford, OX1 1QS
www.theway.org.uk

Cover Design: Paula Nolan

British Library Cataloguing-in-Publication Data
A catalogue record for this book is available
from the British Library

ISBN 978 0 904717 38 9

CONTENTS

Abbreviations   viii

Preface   ix
Joseph A. Munitiz SJ

1. From the Personal to the Corporate   1

2. Discerning and Nurturing a Vocation   24

3. An Apostolic Lifestyle under Vows   55

4. The Longed-for Sending   81

5. Union of the Dispersed   103

6. Governance as Providence   123

7. Towards the Future in Hope   144

Index   164

To Joseph Veale SJ (1921–2002)

mentor and friend

ABBREVIATIONS

AHSI	*Archivum Historicum Societatis Iesu*
Autobiography	*A Pilgrim's Journey: The Autobiography of Ignatius of Loyola,* introduction, translation and commentary by Joseph N. Tylenda (Collegeville: Liturgical, 1991)
CIS	Centrum Ignatianum Spiritualis
Constitutions	in *The Constitutions of the Society of Jesus and Their Complementary Norms* (St Louis: Institute of Jesuit Sources, 1996)
Deliberation	*Deliberation of the First Fathers,* in John C. Futrell, *Making an Apostolic Community of Love: The Role of the Superior according to St Ignatius of Loyola* (St Louis: Institute of Jesuit Sources, 1970), appendix 1, 188–194
Exx	*The Spiritual Exercises of Saint Ignatius,* translated by George E. Ganss (Chicago: Loyola UP, 1992)
Ignatius, *Letters*	*Ignatius of Loyola: Letters and Instructions,* edited by Martin E. Palmer, John W. Padberg and John L. McCarthy (St Louis: Institute of Jesuit Sources, 2006)
Jesuit Life and Mission Today	*Jesuit Life and Mission Today: The Decrees and Accompanying Documents of the 31st – 35th General Congregations of the Society of Jesus* (St Louis: Institute of Jesuit Sources, 2009)
MHSJ	*Monumenta Historica Societatis Jesu,* 157 volumes (Madrid and Rome: Institutum Historicum Societatis Iesu, 1898–)

	Const.	*Constitutiones Societatis Iesu*
	EI	*S. Ignatii epistolae*
	FN	*Fontes narrativi*
	MN	*Monumenta Nadal*

Spiritual Diary	in Ignatius of Loyola, *Personal Writings,* translated by Philip Endean and Joseph A. Munitiz (London: Penguin, 1996)

PREFACE

IGNATIUS CLEARLY GAVE great importance to the *Constitutions*. He felt that one of his major duties when elected Superior General of the newly founded Society of Jesus was to compose a suitable text. His *Spiritual Diary* bears witness to the serious nature of the undertaking: for forty days he struggles to discover the 'will of God' with regard to one particular point of the 'Institute',[1] and in the process is granted his most dramatic series of Trinitarian visions and revelations:

> I had very many intuitions about the Blessed Trinity, my understanding being enlightened with them to such an extent that it seemed to me that with hard study I would not have known so much.[2]

He seems to have been convinced that it had fallen to him to follow in the steps of the great founders of religious orders, and at first may have thought that God would almost dictate to him the decisions he should take. He learnt the hard way that God was in fact expecting something different from him: it would be his duty to use his reason and mental gifts in the laborious task of producing something that sprang from tradition—and hence his careful study, helped by his learned secretary, Juan de Polanco, of other foundation documents—while opening up a completely new vision of what a religious order might be. The result is the document explored with such care and insight by Brian O'Leary in the present book.

The actual writing of the *Constitutions* occupied some six years from 1544; and by the time of the Jubilee Year, 1550, Ignatius had a first draft available. However, it is typical of his 'way of proceeding' that he did not then regard the process as ended. In 1551 he wrote to one of the First Companions, Fr Simão Rodrigues, in Lisbon, informing him that the final revision and publication of the *Constitutions* was not complete.[3]

---

[1] Ironically this concerned the acceptance of a fixed income for the upkeep of a church, a point of relatively minor importance in the overall scheme of the future document.
[2] *Spiritual Diary*, 82.
[3] Ignatius to Rodrigues, 1 December 1551, MHSJ EI 4, 5–9.

In 1553 Jerónimo Nadal (in many ways Ignatius' right-hand man since 1545), was sent to Portugal 'to explain the Society's *Constitutions*'.[4] Ignatius seems to have had little faith in the printed word as the most reliable form of communication. He believed in the key importance of word of mouth, and it is not surprising that 'conversation' has a prominent place[5] in the Jesuit pastoral programme.[6]

It must be admitted that the final text of the *Constitutions* is not an easy one to read: well known (and mentioned in chapter 1) is the reaction of another First Companion, Nicolás de Bobadilla, who complained that they were 'a labyrinth'.[7] As a foundation document it certainly differs greatly from such classical texts as those of St Benedict, St Francis of Assisi and, in our own day, Frère Roger of Taizé. But over the centuries since its composition there have been certain persons, even outside the Society of Jesus, gifted with outstanding insight (such as Mary Ward, the founder of the Institute of the Blessed Virgin Mary), who could appreciate the scope and prophetic value of the *Constitutions*. Today a book like the present one, with its clear presentation of the spiritual principles that underlie the text, provides an immense service. How appropriate that Brian O'Leary has called his book *Explorations*! The reader will find in him a sure guide, already distinguished by his contributions to Ignatian spirituality,[8] who leads us into a territory of immense spiritual depth and richness. This journey will open up a challenging vista for further personal exploration.

Joseph A. Munitiz SJ

---

[4]   Ignatius, *Letters*, 427.
[5]   For example *Constitutions* VII. 4. 8 [648]; see 9 and 110 below.
[6]   See John W. O'Malley, *The First Jesuits* (Cambridge, Ma: Harvard UP, 1993), 110–114.
[7]   MHSJ MN 4, 101 and 733.
[8]   Numerous articles in *The Way*, dating from 1972.

I.

FROM THE PERSONAL TO THE CORPORATE

T HE STORY OF THE JESUIT *CONSTITUTIONS* is part of the story
of Ignatius Loyola. The *Constitutions* are not extrinsic to who
he was, just as *Paradise Lost* is not extrinsic to who John Milton
was. That epic poem could only have been written by Milton
and the *Constitutions* by Ignatius. What is at issue in both cases
is a uniqueness of experience, sensibility and vision that then
finds expression in the written word. Hence we need to know
Ignatius or, more precisely, something of his inner journey, to
be able to enter into the world of the *Constitutions*. Conversely
the *Constitutions*, when read with empathy and understanding,
reveal much of the essence of Ignatius himself. It is not only
in the passage on 'The kind of person the Superior General
should be' that a portrait of Ignatius can be detected in the
Constitutions.[1]

Interpreting the *Acta*

In recent years students of Ignatian history and spirituality have
relied heavily on the document that is generally referred to in
English as the *Autobiography*. This is now a preferred source,
being a first-hand account by the saint himself of his life from
1521 (the siege of Pamplona) to 1538 (the year after his arrival in
Rome). The growing familiarity of the *Autobiography* has been
largely responsible for changing the image of Ignatius from that

---

[1] *Constitutions* IX. 2. 1–10 [723–735]. This chapter 2 of part IX has often been regarded
as an unconscious self-portrait by Ignatius. In his *Memoriale*, Luís Gonçalves da Câmara
writes of how he sees incarnated in Ignatius the rules of the *Spiritual Exercises* and the
teachings of *The Imitation of Christ*. Then he adds: 'The same can be said about the
Constitutions, especially the chapter in which he portrays the General, in which he
seems to have painted a portrait of himself' (n. 226, in *Remembering Iñigo: Glimpses of
the Life of Saint Ignatius of Loyola: The Memoriale of Luís Gonçalves da Câmara*,
translated with introduction, notes and indices by Alexander Eaglestone and Joseph A.
Munitiz [Leominster: Gracewing and St Louis: Institute of Jesuit Sources, 2004], 131).
Further discussion will be found in chapter 6.

of a soldier-saint to that of a mystic. It has encouraged directors
of the Spiritual Exercises to interpret them less ascetically and more
contemplatively. Ignatius himself has become more accessible
through his revealing of his foibles and struggles as well as his
mystical graces. The *Autobiography* offers us a more rounded
picture of the man, softening his severe image and making him
more human.

But is this text, originally entitled simply *Acta*,[2] really an
autobiography? Have we been too simplistic in our interpretation
and use of it? Such is the view of Marjorie O'Rourke Boyle
when she writes, 'The premise of modern interpretation is that
this "life" is an autobiographical narrative as a factually historical
document'.[3] Boyle, a cultural historian specialising in the rhetoric
of religion, brings a strong hermeneutic of suspicion to her
reading of the text. She rightly explores the complicated way in
which, through the mediation of Luís Gonçalves da Câmara and
various scribes, the text as we have it emerged. She writes:

> *Acta* is not autobiography. Loyola, unlike Augustine, did not
> even compose the text. It was five times removed from his
> lips: after recital were audition, memorisation, notation,
> composition, transcription.[4]

Boyle displays an encyclopaedic knowledge of the sixteenth
century and its culture in her book. Her insights are fascinating
and cannot but enrich our reading of the *Acta*. But in attributing
'historical literalism' to the way other authors interpret this
text she is overstating her case. Hardly anyone considers it as
autobiography in the strict sense. Hence even when authors use
the word it is simply for the sake of convenience or tradition
(even if that tradition is mostly confined to the English-speaking
world and only reaches back to the first US translation in
1900).[5] But there is certainly a historical core in the document,

[2] Luís Gonçalves da Câmara, *Acta patris ignatii*, edited by Dionisio Fernandez Zapico
and Candido de Dalmases, MHSJ FN 1, 323–507.
[3] Marjorie O'Rourke Boyle, *Loyola's Acts: The Rhetoric of the Self* (Berkeley and Los
Angeles: U. of California P, 1997), 2.
[4] Boyle, *Loyola's Acts*, 3–4.
[5] *The Autobiography of St Ignatius*, translated by J. F. X. O'Connor (New York:
Benzinger, 1900).

however indirectly that core has been mediated to us, and however puzzling the document's literary genre may be. For Boyle, 'The text is epideictic rhetoric, in conformity with Loyola's determination in his *Exercitia spiritualia* of the primary purpose of life as epideictic: "to praise" God'.[6] This interpretation does not in itself exclude autobiographical truth. Indeed Boyle herself makes many statements that show that she is willing to draw historical, and even psychological, conclusions from the text. For example:

> The intriguing man is the self who walks off the pages of the text in 1537—the Loyola who by 1553 is able to review his experience critically, but with humor rather than the hatred he conceived against himself during convalescence. He has matured beyond simple disgust for sin, as in the *Exercitia spiritualia*, where the penitent is to meditate upon himself as just plain filthy.[7]

So we *can* learn about Ignatius, and particularly about his inner life, from this text![8]

Purpose of the Narrative

Ignatius experienced, and expressed, great reluctance to tell his life story.[9] The reasons were partly ill health, partly the pressure of important and urgent work, and partly a lingering fear of vainglory (the endemic temptation of a person steeped in chivalry). But his closest companions, including his secretary Polanco[10]

---

[6] Boyle, *Loyola's Acts*, 3.

[7] Boyle, *Loyola's Acts*, 182. She mistakes the date—it should be 1538.

[8] Another author who comes to the text from a background in cultural studies is Peter du Brul, in his *Ignatius: Sharing the Pilgrim Story. A Reading of the Autobiography of St Ignatius of Loyola* (Leominster: Gracewing, 2003). His methodology, however, is significantly different from Boyle's.

[9] My reflections on the Autobiography, here somewhat adapted, were first published as 'The Autobiography of St Ignatius', *Spirituality*, 6/31 (2000), 214–217, and 6/32 (2000), 280–283.

[10] Juan Afonso de Polanco (1517–1576), a native of Burgos, was a graduate of the University of Paris and held the post of notary in the Papal Curia. He joined the Society in 1541 and became Ignatius' secretary in 1547. He made a major contribution to the composition of the *Constitutions*.

and especially Nadal,[11] were insistent in pressing him. Eventually he did as he was asked. Of great importance are the reasons why his contemporaries were so anxious to have him relate his life story. Fortunately, the two Prologues, one written by Gonçalves da Câmara and the other by Nadal, throw light on the matter.[12] Let us turn first to Nadal:

> Since I knew that the holy father-founders of monastic communities had been accustomed to leave their sons some admonition, as a testament, to help them grow in virtue, I waited for the opportune moment to ask the same of Father Ignatius.[13]

The key word here is 'testament'. Like the *Testament of Francis of Assisi*,[14] the hoped-for Ignatian document was to have as its purpose the guidance and encouragement of the family that Ignatius was to leave behind him at his death. It was to be a way for him to live on in that family, for his spirit to be incarnated in future generations of followers.

Further on in the same Prologue, Nadal writes:

> Thinking that this was the suitable moment, I begged the Father to be kind enough to tell us how the Lord had guided him from the beginning of his conversion, so that his explanation could serve us as a testament and paternal instruction.[15]

We note here, besides the repetition of the word 'testament', the even more precise spelling out of what was being asked: that Ignatius would tell the story of God's initiative and involvement in his life. Nadal kept returning to this key issue in different

---

[11] Jerónimo Nadal (1507–1580) studied in Alcalá, Paris and Avignon. After much inner turmoil he entered the Society in 1545. A man of immense talent, Ignatius gradually made him a trusted confidant. He played a key role in the promulgation of the *Constitutions*.

[12] Quotations from these Prologues are taken from *A Pilgrim's Journey: The Autobiography of Ignatius of Loyola*, introduction, translation and commentary by Joseph N. Tylenda (Collegeville: Liturgical, 1991).

[13] Tylenda, *Pilgrim's Journey*, 123.

[14] English translation in *Francis and Clare: The Complete Works*, translated with an introduction by Regis J. Armstrong and Ignatius C. Brady (Ramsey, NJ: Paulist, 1982), 154–156.

[15] Tylenda, *Pilgrim's Journey*, 123.

ways, stressing its crucial importance for the Society of Jesus. In another place he writes: 'The Society develops in the same ways as the life of our Father unfolded'.[16] This statement parallels yet another that is attributed to Nadal by da Câmara in his own Prologue:

> When Father Nadal arrived he was very happy to see that the project was begun and told me to urge the Father to continue, telling me many times that the Father could do nothing better for the Society than this, and that this was to give the Society's true foundations.[17]

This last phrase reads in Spanish: '*y que esto era fundar verdaderamente la Compañía*'. This is an extremely strong assertion that almost puts the *Autobiography* on the same level of importance as the *Formula of the Institute* and the *Constitutions!*[18] Nadal is sometimes prone to exaggeration, but the thinking behind this statement seems to have been shared by Ignatius, for according to Diego Laínez:

> Father Ignatius used to say that when God chooses someone to be the founder of a religious order, he leads him in such a way as he wishes those who follow him to walk also.[19]

Seen against the background of his companions' expectations, it may well be that the long delay before Ignatius finally told his story, even his own hesitations and misgivings, and the constant and irritating postponements, all brought some advantage. These factors probably induced him to spend more time in prayerful remembering through which he could better distil the essence of his religious experience. There is in the *Autobiography* an obvious selectivity. While some of this may have been unconscious

---

[16] MHSJ FN 2, 9.

[17] Tylenda, *Pilgrim's Journey*, 4–5.

[18] Work on the *Constitutions* was substantially complete in 1551. This was part of the context for Nadal's request to Ignatius to tell his story. The time sequence lends weight to an argument that the *Autobiography* is closely linked with the *Constitutions*, explaining their roots, or highlighting the spirit in which they are to be lived, or as commentary. See p. 6 for comment on Nadal's view of Ignatius as the sole founder of the Society.

[19] Anonymous author of *Vita patris nostri Ignatii*, MHSJ FN 2, 428. This statement is also found in Diego Laínez, *Adhortationes* (1559), MHSJ FN 2, 137.

or due to forgetfulness, most was probably careful and deliberate, the result of discernment. Ignatius was not interested in merely relating external facts, most of which would have been well known already, at least to his closest companions. His aim was to offer an *interpretation* of his life's experience (how God had led him) from the perspective of his own mature faith vision, and in so doing to present a tangible *model* for Jesuits to follow (since God will lead them in the same way as he led Ignatius).

It is difficult to overestimate the role of Nadal in propagating this account of Jesuit origins. Having prodded Ignatius to tell his story, he then used that narrative to create a theology of Jesuit life and an image of Ignatius as the sole founder of the Society of Jesus. Nadal's interpretation is not without its problems. John O'Malley writes:

> Nadal, Ignatius's peripatetic and plenipotentiary agent to Jesuit communities across Europe, used this account [the *Autobiography*] for almost twenty years to tell Jesuits what it meant to be a Jesuit. Ignatius was the paradigm for every member of the Society. The image that Ignatius provided of himself is without question the basis for the image Nadal constructed and infused into the traditions of the Society, but Nadal went beyond it in several ways. Portraying Ignatius as a man guided by the direct inspiration of God, he saw him in this regard as the modern equivalent of founders of great religious orders like St Dominic and St Francis of Assisi. In doing so Nadal slighted the role played in the founding by the companions who joined Ignatius at Paris, and his neglect of their contribution resulted in a tendency strongly operative even today to attribute to Ignatius all the important features discernible in the early formation of the Society's character. This has meant a more monolithic image of the Society's origin and development than the documentation warrants.[20]

[20] John W. O'Malley, 'The Historiography of the Society of Jesus', in *The Jesuits: Cultures, Sciences, and the Arts, 1540–1773*, edited by John W. O'Malley and others (U. of Toronto P, 1999), 3–37, here 5. Nadal's stance contributed to the difficulties of Nicolás Bobadilla, which climaxed in the critical years 1556–1558. For an account that differs from that of most Jesuit authors, and is quite sympathetic to Bobadilla, see Arthur L. Fisher, 'A Study in Early Jesuit Government: The Nature and Origins of the Dissent of Nicolás Bobadilla', *Viator*, 10 (1979), 397–431.

Towards an Apostolic Spirituality

One of the key developments that we find in the *Autobiography* might be described as a move 'from asceticism to apostolate'. In the immediate aftermath of his conversion experience at Loyola Ignatius retained a searing consciousness of his sins, out of which grew a great desire to do penance and make atonement. He began to practise a spirituality of great, indeed extreme, asceticism. His models were the Desert Fathers, whose lives he had read in the *Flos sanctorum.* Among them was Onuphrius, an Egyptian hermit who had let his hair grow until his entire body was covered![21] But even while living this ascetical spirituality Ignatius found that his inner motivation was gradually changing away from its penitential origins towards a desire to do something pleasing to God. This motivational change was already an initial step forward out of self-centredness.

Nevertheless, the spirituality of both these stages was primarily focused on his own efforts and his own needs. There was a narcissistic element at its core. It was finding expression in the chivalric ideal of the knight who performs great deeds. Ignatius wanted to distinguish himself by his labours and so win acclaim from God. There was no awareness, or at least no articulated awareness, of a call to ministry or service.

Yet even while he was still convalescing at Loyola he had practised some outreach to others. 'During the time he spent talking to the members of the household he spoke about the things of God and he thus brought much profit to their souls.' (*Autobiography*, n. 11) This memory remained with him, but at the time the implications of the experience did not impinge on him. He did not see its significance as a pointer to the future and it did not lead him to any decision. He was too immersed in his chivalric dreams. The real breakthrough happened after he had become a pilgrim and had begun to grow in spiritual sensitivity.

> It was likewise in Manresa—where he stayed for almost a year, and after experiencing divine consolations and seeing

---

[21] See *Paphnutius: Histories of the Monks of Upper Egypt and the Life of Onophrius,* translated by Tim Vivian (Kalamazoo: Cistercian Publications, 1993), 143–166.

> the fruits that he was bringing forth in the souls he was
> helping—that he abandoned those extremes he had
> previously practised and began to cut his nails and hair.
> (*Autobiography*, n. 29)

Now he is paying attention, not only to what is happening
within himself, but also to what is happening in others with whom
he enters into spiritual conversation. Instead of performing great
deeds for God (and so focusing on himself) he is drawn to bring
forth fruit in others (and so give glory to God). This is a
breakthrough moment and it leads to decision. If he is to help
others Onuphrius is no longer an adequate model!

What makes his reference to these conversations at Manresa
so remarkable is its context. Ignatius inserts it into the narrative
of the deep mystical graces he was receiving at that time: a vision
of the Trinity, a new understanding of creation, an enlightenment
on the Eucharist, a vision of the humanity of Christ, a vision of
Our Lady, and the culmination—the 'great enlightenment' on
the banks of the Cardoner.[22] To speak about cutting his nails
and hair in the middle of such delicate self-disclosure may seem
like descending into bathos. Yet the two realities are intimately
connected: the soaring vision and the ludicrously humble detail.
Ignatius is discovering an important key to apostolic spirituality,
to the dynamic of contemplation and action.

We might summarise the connections and the sequence of
the inner movements that Ignatius experienced as follows:

- Through the mystical favours he has been receiving Ignatius
  is led into consolation.

- In the assurance and light of this consolation he has the
  sensibility not only to notice the fruit he is bringing forth
  in others, but also to begin to grasp the far-reaching
  implications of this phenomenon.

- This sensibility also brings a realisation that God is more
  pleased and better served by a person's helping others to
  find God than by a life of austerity in itself.

---

[22] See *Autobiography*, nn. 28–30. A lengthy discussion of the Cardoner experience will
appear in chapter 7.

- In order to help others most effectively he sees that a person needs to be approachable, affable, and unexceptional in appearance, manner and dress.

Where Will This Lead?

Such was the dynamic of Ignatius' first phase in explicitly espousing an apostolic spirituality. This is not to claim that he had never before reflected on the apostolic life. He had admired Francis and Dominic, whose lives he had read in the *Flos sanctorum* during his convalescence. But they had mostly attracted him because of their 'great deeds' which he then yearned to emulate.[23] He had not yet been grasped by their evangelizing zeal. This did not capture his imagination at Loyola. It was only in the consolation of his mystical experiences at Manresa that he was able to grasp the vital link, indeed the equivalence, between the glory of God, the service of God and loving outreach to other people.

From that moment onwards he was never merely a pilgrim, but a pilgrim who was always on the lookout for opportunities to evangelize. His chosen method, marked by a great simplicity, was spiritual conversation; and the apex of such conversation was to become the Spiritual Exercises.[24] To the desire 'to save his soul' was added the desire 'to help souls', and the two desires were never again to be considered apart. The lifestyle that Ignatius was beginning to evolve needed to concretise and express these desires—not one now and the other later, not one at the expense of the other, not even one subordinate to the other— but both together, at one and the same time, inseparably.

So far we have been considering Ignatius the individual and his discovery of a spirituality that would break through the limitations of a narrow concern for his own personal relationship with God and reach out to embrace the 'other'. Since the chief

[23] 'Throughout these thoughts he used to say to himself: "Saint Dominic did this, so I have to do it too. Saint Francis did this, so I have to do it too."' (*Autobiography*, n.7)
[24] See Thomas H. Clancy, *The Conversational Word of God: A Commentary on the Doctrine of St Ignatius of Loyola Concerning Spiritual Conversation* (St Louis: Institute of Jesuit Sources, 1978).

means to this outreach was spiritual conversation, the 'other' tended at first to be confined to those relatively few individuals who crossed his path in his early wanderings. But gradually the meaning of the 'other' expanded in line with his expanding apostolic horizon. This horizon was being shaped by his contemplative experiences. The more Ignatius was drawn, through prayer, into the inner life of the Trinity, the more he began to see what they saw:

> Here it is how the three Divine Persons gazed on the whole surface or circuit of the world, full of people (Exx 102).

> Some white and others black, some in peace, and others at war, some weeping and others laughing, some healthy and others sick, some being born and others dying, and so forth (Exx 106).

And the more he saw and reflected on what the Trinity saw, the more he desired what they desired: 'Let us work the redemption of the human race' (Exx 107).

Gathering Companions

This universal vision was energizing, stimulating, challenging. But it soon dawned on Ignatius that one person alone could only make a very minor contribution to this venture, no matter how generous and energetic he might be. However, what if others could be brought to share his vision and join him in the project? In the exercise on the Call of the King he wrote:

> [Christ] calls them all, and to each person in particular he says: 'My will is to conquer the whole world and all my enemies, and thus to enter into the glory of my Father. Therefore, whoever wishes to come with me must labour with me, so that through following me in the pain he or she may follow me also in the glory' (Exx 95).

If this is indeed true, and the call is addressed to all and to each one in particular, then there is a real possibility of bringing together a group of like-minded and dedicated companions who *together* would give their lives to help fulfil the desires of the Trinity for humankind.

Hence came the early and ultimately unsuccessful efforts of Ignatius to gather followers in Spain. It was only at the University of Paris that he eventually met the young men who, through sharing their faith, prayer, studies and recreation, and especially through their experience of the Spiritual Exercises, formed themselves into an informal *compañía* or fellowship of 'friends in the Lord'.[25] Through these years of philosophical and theological studies they were developing what they chose to call 'our way of proceeding'. This phrase was shorthand for a whole way of life: a spirituality and an evolving lifestyle that would incarnate that spirituality. It emerged from what they had learnt from making the Spiritual Exercises and was centred on the practice of discernment.

Jerusalem attracted the companions like a magnet, as it had Ignatius during his conversion. They planned to go there after graduation but were realistic enough to acknowledge that this might not be possible. So in the vows that they took on Montmartre in 1534 they stipulated that, in the event of not being able to travel to, or remain in, the Holy Land, they would put themselves at the service of the Pope.[26] Ignatius succinctly says:

> By this time they had all decided on what they would do, that is, go to Venice and Jerusalem, and spend their lives there helping souls, and if permission be not granted them to remain in Jerusalem, they would return to Rome and offer themselves to the Vicar of Christ so that he could use them wherever he judged it would be for the greater glory of God and the good of souls (*Autobiography*, n. 85).[27]

When they arrived in Venice they discovered that their fears were well grounded, as no pilgrim ships were sailing because of the war between Venice and the Turks. They decided to give

<hr>

[25] Ignatius uses this phrase in a letter from Venice in 1537: 'In mid-January nine friends of mine in the Lord arrived here from Paris', Ignatius, *Letters*, 29.
[26] See *CIS*, 49, *The Montmartre Vows: History and Spirituality* (1985).
[27] Where Ignatius gives the impression that everyone in the group felt the same way, Polanco makes clear that there were differences of opinion about what to do in the Holy Land, especially on the question of whether to remain there for the rest of their lives or to return to Europe after a period (*Summarium hispanum de origine et progressu Societatis Iesu* [1547/1548], MHSJ FN 1, 185).

themselves one year in hope of peace coming to the Mediterranean. Meanwhile they received priestly ordination in June 1537. Then they had a communal experience of sharing for some months a life of prayer and ministry in small groups in some of the towns of northern Italy.[28]

Later that same year the mystique or deeper spiritual meaning of their apostolic companionship was communicated to Ignatius while travelling to Rome. This revelation is known as the vision of La Storta.

> After he had been ordained a priest, he decided to wait another year before celebrating Mass, preparing himself and praying to our Lady to place him with her Son. One day, a few miles before reaching Rome, while praying in a church, he felt a great change in his soul and so clearly did he see God the Father place him with Christ, His Son, that he had no doubts that God the Father did place him with His Son. (*Autobiography*, n.96)

While on his journey, with Favre and Laínez, Ignatius had been praying the colloquy of the Two Standards meditation in the Exercises (concentrating apparently on petitioning Our Lady), and at La Storta he had received the grace he asked for.

As so often, Ignatius merely gives the basic fact and omits all detail and embellishment. But from those who were with him we learn that as soon as Ignatius entered the church (it was really a small, dilapidated chapel) he felt a sudden change come over him. He saw God the Father, together with Jesus who was carrying his cross. Both Father and Son were looking most kindly on him and he heard the Father say to the Son: 'I wish you to take this man as your servant'. Jesus then directed his words to the kneeling pilgrim and said, 'I wish you to be our servant'. This was what Ignatius had always wanted. Then he heard the Father add, 'I will be favourable to you [plural] in Rome'. Whether this promise meant success or persecution Ignatius was unsure, but he knew for certain that the Lord would be with him.[29]

---

[28] This experience, a mix of withdrawal, community living and ministry, became the model for the Jesuit Third Probation or Tertianship.

[29] The details of the vision, not found in the *Autobiography*, come mainly from Nadal, *Exhortationes in Hispania* (1554), MHSJ FN 1, 313–314, and Laínez, *Adhortationes in*

Offering to the Pope

Although Ignatius was the only person who had this experience, he immediately interpreted it as applying to his companions as well. He was aware that not only he, but all the 'friends in the Lord' had been placed with Christ. They too had received the promise; they too were being drawn into an ongoing experience of the paschal mystery. From then on Ignatius had a deeper sense of the corporate dimension of his own call, his own mission, and perhaps a premonition of the reality to which he would subsequently refer in the *Constitutions* as 'the body'.[30] But that development was still a few years off. Meanwhile the companions had to continue exploring possibilities as they all gathered together in Rome. This they did, and in the following year (1538) they formally offered their services to the Pope for priestly ministry anywhere in the world.

Some have interpreted this action of the companions as consciously taking a polemical, anti-Lutheran stance. Of course they accepted traditional Roman Catholic teaching on the role of the Pope in the Church and regarded him as the Vicar of Christ. But at this point they were surprisingly naïve concerning the theological controversies of the era. In spite of being exposed to Lutheran ideas at the University of Paris they seem not to have grasped their theological power. Even after some bruising encounters with the Reformers during their journey from Paris to Venice (to join Ignatius) in 1536–1537,[31] the companions continued to underestimate the profound changes that were taking place in the Church. So in offering their services to the Pope their motivation was far more practical than theological, more

---

librum Examinis (1559), MHSJ FN 2, 133. Nadal makes several references elsewhere to its meaning for Ignatius and the Society. See also Hugo Rahner, *The Vision of St Ignatius in the Chapel of La Storta* (Rome: CIS, 1975); Peter-Hans Kolvenbach, 'Introduction: The Vision at La Storta', in Kolvenbach, *The Road from La Storta* (St Louis: Institute of Jesuit Sources, 2000), 1–4.

[30] See Rogelio García-Mateo, '"The Body of the Society": Its Understanding in the Sixteenth-Century Socio-Religious Context, and its Meaning for Today', *CIS*, 66, 'Omnia intelligendo iuxta Constitutiones', part 2 (1991), 11–24.

[31] See *A Brief and Exact Account: The Recollections of Simão Rodrigues on the Origin and Progress of the Society of Jesus,* translated with an introduction and commentary by Joseph F. Conwell (St Louis: Institute of Jesuit Sources, 2004), 36–43.

pastoral than polemical. It had nothing directly to do with the Reformation.[32] They simply wanted to evangelize, to minister in areas of greatest need. Because of his position, the Pope was the person most aware of where those needs were.

Pierre Favre wrote in a letter, on behalf of all the companions, to Diego de Gouveia[33] that same year: 'The reason why we have thus put ourselves under his [the Pope's] judgment and will is the knowledge that he is better acquainted with the needs of the whole of Christendom'.[34] This simple statement is filled out more authoritatively in the *Constitutions*:

> For those who first united to form the Society were from different provinces and realms and did not know into which regions they were to go, whether among the faithful or the unbelievers; and therefore, to avoid erring in the path of the Lord, they made that promise or vow in order that His Holiness might distribute them for the greater glory of God (VII.1.B[605]).

So at this juncture in their history, who were these 'friends in the Lord'? They were a group of priests, ordained *ad titulum paupertatis voluntarie et sufficientis litteraturae*[35] and so not incardinated in any particular diocese, educated above the average for clerics of that period, leading upright lives, devoted to pastoral ministry, and so regarded by their contemporaries as *preti riformati* (reformed priests),[36] totally available to the Pope for

---

[32] Nadal was later to bring an anti-Lutheran interpretation to Jesuit origins and the *Constitutions*. See Jos E. Vercruysse, 'Nadal and the Counter-Reformation: An Anti-Protestant Interpretation of the *Constitutions*?' *CIS*, 65, '*Omnia Intelligendo iuxta Constitutiones*', part 1 (1990), 80–90.

[33] A Portuguese, he was rector of the Collège Sainte Barbe when Favre enrolled there in 1525.

[34] MHSJ EI 1, 132.

[35] 'Under the title of voluntary poverty and sufficient learning', the words of the Papal *motu proprio* allowing the companions to be ordained. As priests they would have the freedom of movement that they desired, not having pastoral responsibility for any local community. See Polanco, *Summarium hispanum*, n.68, MHSJ FN 1, 192.

[36] Italians used this designation for priests who were committed to reform and showed it by simplicity of lifestyle and care for their pastoral responsibilities. Mark A. Lewis interprets the phrase more corporately, seeing it as referring to groups of priests such as the Theatines, Barnabites and Somaschans. *Preti riformati* would then be the popular equivalent for the ecclesiastical term *clerici regolari*, clerks regular. The companions had friendly dealings with such priests in northern Italy in 1538. See Lewis, 'The First Jesuits as "Reformed Priests"', *AHSI*, 65 (1996), 111–127.

any kind of apostolic ministry throughout the world, and relying on him to be aware of the areas of greatest need. It was only when the Pope took them at their word and began to disperse them on missions that they were forced to ask questions concerning their continuing relationship with one another. This was the background of a corporate discernment process known as the Deliberation of the First Fathers in 1539.[37]

Two Pivotal Choices

The companions did not gather for this Deliberation in order to begin again their search for the will of God. They entered the process with basic certainties which they saw no reason to question. For example, the opening paragraph of the record of the Deliberation begins:

> Near the end of Lent the time was drawing near when we would have to be dispersed and separated from one another. We were very eager for this, recognising it as necessary in order to reach the goal we had already fixed upon and thought about with intense desire. (*Deliberation*, n. 1)

So their goal, the purpose and orientation of their lives, was clear. The Deliberation was to be about means. How are we to reach our goal in these new circumstances when the Pope is sending us to different places and we can no longer remain together? Later in the same paragraph we find a similar expression of their inner certainties: 'There was unity of mind and purpose: to seek the gracious and perfect will of God according to the scope of our vocation' (*Deliberation*, n. 1). That 'scope of their vocation' had gradually been clarified and confirmed over the years since they had first come together as 'friends in the Lord', since they had first made the Spiritual Exercises.

The First Fathers, as the companions came to be called, faced two main questions during this Deliberation. The first concerned their relationships with each other. Granted the way in which the Pope had decided to mission them,

---

[37] The document that records these deliberations has a notation in Ignatius' own handwriting: '1539. During three months. The manner to structure interiorly [*ordenarse*] the Society.' (MHSJ Const. 1, xxxv)

> ... would it be better for us to be so joined and bound together in one body that no physical dispersal, however great, could separate us? Or perhaps would this be inexpedient? (*Deliberation*, n. 3)

The decision was easily made in favour of the first alternative:

> ... that since the most kind and loving Lord had deigned to unite us to one another and to bring us together ... we should not sever God's union and bringing together, but rather everyday we should strengthen and more solidly ground it, forming ourselves into one body (*Deliberation*, n. 3).

Their companionship and friendship are God's gift to them, to be treasured and fostered, but with the realisation that this gift is not so much an end in itself as a vibrant source of apostolic energy. And so:

> ... everyone should have concern for and comprehension of the others for greater apostolic efficacy, since united strength would have more power and courage in confronting whatever challenging goals were to be sought than if this strength were divided into many parts (*Deliberation*, n. 3).

This decision appears at first sight to be highly paradoxical: there is an eagerness to sacrifice their union or companionship through dispersal, while at the same time maintaining and strengthening it. Of course, what they were really sacrificing was one particular experience and expression of companionship, namely that of physical presence or closeness to one another. This was not the same as abandoning their bond of union, but it left them with the challenge as to how to keep and even deepen that bond in other ways than through physical proximity.

Here we encounter a crucial constituent of corporate apostolic spirituality, a constituent that produces a particular kind of tension within the individual member and within the group or body to which he or she belongs. This tension is between the polarities of union and mission, to both of which the apostolic person or group is committed. These polarities do not sit comfortably together. They tend to pull a person or group in opposite directions.

Ignatius and his companions are already experiencing the tension as they begin the Deliberation, and later the issue will pervade the *Constitutions*.[38] But in both documents two principles are established. The first is that the companions must live with the tension rather than attempt to dissolve it (for example by choosing one polarity at the expense of the other). The second is that there is an order within the polarities, namely that the good or value that is union is in service of the greater good that is mission. The two are interlinked, are even interdependent, but for an apostolic group or body such as the Society of Jesus mission will always be the final end and be given the ultimate priority. Union will express itself in mission.

The answer to this first question on union led into the further question of the kind of structure this union would have.

> We now asked ourselves whether we should pronounce a third vow, namely to obey one of us in order that we might carry out the will of our Lord God more sincerely ... and at the same time carry out the will and command of His Holiness (*Deliberation*, n.4).

The companions' answer to this would determine whether or not they would become a religious order. They were already committed to poverty and celibacy.[39] Would they now also make a vow of obedience to someone within the group, and so canonically become religious?

This second question proved much more intractable than the first. They even had to change their method of discernment midstream, so difficult was it to reach a conclusion.[40] The text of the *Deliberation* gives some of the reasons raised by the companions for and against becoming a religious order. It was by no means obvious how the discernment would end. However, they finally reached a conclusion 'not just by a majority but

---

[38] This tension is explicitly acknowledged in part VIII, which will be reflected on in chapter 5.

[39] These were included in the vows at Montmartre in 1534. See Polanco, *Summarium italicum de origine et progressu Societatis Iesu* (1549–1551), MHSJ FN 1, 263. Before ordination in 1537 the companions again pronounced vows of poverty and chastity before the Nuncio Varallo. See Ignatius' *Autobiography*, n.93 and Polanco, *Summarium hispanum*, MHSJ FN 1, 193.

[40] A helpful discussion of this change of method is that by Jules J. Toner in 'The Deliberation that Started the Jesuits: A Commentary on the *Deliberatio Primorum Patrum*', *Studies in the Spirituality of Jesuits*, 6/4 (1974), 193–208.

without even one dissenting'. In all communal discernment
the hope is that consensus will emerge and the matter need not
be decided by majority vote. This hope was fulfilled for the
companions. Their decision was:

> ... that it would be more expedient, and even necessary, to
> vow obedience to one of our companions in order that we
> might better and more exactly fulfil our principal desires of
> accomplishing the divine will in all things, and in order
> that the Society might be more surely preserved in being,
> and finally, that all individual matters that might occur,
> both spiritual and temporal, might be provided for properly
> (*Deliberation*, n. 8).

The Spiritual Exercises teach that, after any decision seeking to
respond to the will of God, confirmation should be asked for. In
the case of the First Fathers such confirmation came interiorly
through the experience of harmony and joy that accompanied
their consensus. Exteriorly, confirmation came through the
approbation of the *Formula of the Institute* by Paul III in the
Bull *Regimini militantis ecclesiae* in the following year (1540).[41]
This Formula (which corresponds to the Rule in older orders)
incorporated a document entitled 'The First Sketch of the Institute'
which was composed by Ignatius to express the nature and identity
of the new body.[42] The Pope gave his approval to this identity.

Constitutions for the Body

The Formula gave the Superior General the authority to draw up
Constitutions in consultation with the other companions.[43] The

---

[41] This interpretation of interior and exterior confirmation is widely accepted. However, a
dissenting view, strongly argued, is found in Jules J. Toner, *Discerning God's Will:
Ignatius of Loyola's Teaching on Christian Decision Making* (St Louis: Institute of Jesuit
Sources, 1991), chapters 11 and 12.

[42] For a wide-ranging discussion see *The Formula of the Institute* with articles by Antonio
M. de Aldama, Georges Bottereau, Mario Gioia, Gervais Dumeige, Paolo Dezza and
Luis González (Rome: CIS, 1982). Also de Aldama, *The Formula of the Institute: Notes
for a Commentary* (St Louis: Institute of Jesuit Sources, 1990). There are two versions
of the Formula, that of 1540 and a later one rewritten in the light of experience in 1550.
Quotations will always be from the 1550 text.

[43] 'This Superior General, with the advice of his associates, shall possess the authority to
establish *Constitutions* leading to the achievement of this end which has been proposed
to us, with the majority of votes always having the right to prevail.' (*Formula of the
Institute*, n. 2)

election of a first Superior General became urgent, so the next year six of the First Companions gathered in Rome for that purpose. Ignatius was elected to govern the Society. While they were together, the companions also worked on certain issues that remained unresolved from their 1539 Deliberation. Their decisions became known as the Constitutions of 1541,[44] although they were understood to be provisional. It had already become clear that it would be impossible for all the companions, who were becoming increasingly dispersed, to collaborate on writing fuller *Constitutions*. Even a decision to leave the task to those living in Italy proved unworkable.[45] Hence it became the responsibility of Ignatius alone.

The composition of the *Constitutions* was in progress right up to the death of Ignatius in 1556 and is extremely complex. The details are available in the *Monumenta* and are presented more succinctly in de Aldama's *Commentary*.[46] There is general agreement that the turning-point in the process of composition was the appointment of Polanco as Secretary to the Society in 1547. Before that date, apart from some preparatory documents, Ignatius had only managed to complete a text of the General Examen (1546–1547). Polanco, however, besides the research, organizational and compositional skills that he possessed, also had the time (which Ignatius did not) to devote to the task.

The relationship between Ignatius and Polanco, and the nature of the collaboration between them, have been subjects of much debate.[47] It is obvious that Polanco was much more than a secretary. So who is the author of the *Constitutions*? Is it really an Ignatian document? Here it must suffice to quote the conclusion drawn by de Aldama from his vast erudition on the subject:

---

[44] MHSJ Const. I, 34–48.

[45] MHSJ Const. I, 23–24.

[46] Antonio M. de Aldama, *The Constitutions of the Society of Jesus: An Introductory Commentary on the Constitutions*, translated by Aloysius J. Owen (Rome: CIS and St Louis: Institute of Jesuit Sources, 1989), 2–8.

[47] In recent times this debate was rekindled by François Roustang's introduction to *Constitutions de la Compagnie de Jésus: Introduction à une lecture*, volume 2, translated by François Courel (Paris: Desclée de Brouwer, 1967). See also Roustang, 'Sur le rôle de Polanco dans la rédaction des *Constitutions* S.J.', *Revue d'ascétique et de mystique*, 42/166 (April–June 1966), 193–202.

There is, then, no doubt that the *Constitutions* express the *thought* of Ignatius, though this does not mean that we can analyse each word and sentence as if they were all spoken or written by the saint himself. Only in those passages where the textual history indicates a direct intervention by Ignatius is such analysis justified. In general, the actual words and phrases are the means used by Polanco to express the mind of the founder. Doubtless some, or even many, of them came directly from Ignatius in conversation with his secretary, though we cannot be certain which ones these are.[48]

It is interesting to note that, in spite of the active collaboration of Polanco, Ignatius saw himself as the author of the *Constitutions*. Da Câmara records:

The method he followed when writing the *Constitutions* was to celebrate Mass every day and present the point under consideration to God and to pray over it. He always had tears when he prayed or celebrated Mass. (*Autobiography*, n.101)

This is further borne out in his *Spiritual Diary*, which shows Ignatius struggling with the issue of the kind of poverty most appropriate for the Society of Jesus.[49] The text of the *Constitutions*, however much influenced by Polanco, ultimately grew out of Ignatius' inner experience of God. This experience, while immediately that of his prayer day by day while working on the *Constitutions*, reached back to all that had happened in Manresa. From many texts by the early companions on the Manresa connection I choose one by Nadal.

Ignatius always prized this gift [the Cardoner experience] highly; because of it he conceived a profound modesty and humility; from it there began to shine on his countenance an indescribable spiritual light and alacrity. He was wont to refer to that one grace and light whenever he was questioned either about serious matters or about some reasons for the way of life in the Society—as though he had seen on that one occasion the inner causes and bases of all things.[50]

[48] De Aldama, *Introductory Commentary*, 11.
[49] See Simon Decloux, *Commentaries on the Letters and Spiritual Diary of St Ignatius Loyola* (Rome: CIS, 1982), 80–123.
[50] *Commentarii de Instituto S.I.*, secundus dialogus, MHSJ MN 5, 612.

Continuity and Permanence

Central to any understanding of the *Constitutions* is the recognition that Ignatius (and the early companions) expressly wished to pass on to later generations of Jesuits the particular experience they had shared with one another. Indeed, the two major decisions that had emanated from the Deliberation (that is, to form themselves into one body and to vow obedience to one of themselves) might together be described as an option for continuity and permanence. The First Fathers regarded their own experience over the years since they had come to know Ignatius as their formation, and for Ignatius his time at Manresa had been his novitiate. Formation takes place in the Society of Jesus through a pattern of experience closely similar to that of the early companions and in continuity with it, just as their formation was an experience closely similar to, and in continuity with that of Ignatius. Permanence depends on continuity of experience; continuity of experience is another term for formation.[51] The goals of permanence and unity are expressed quite explicitly in the second *Formula of the Institute* (1550):

> Therefore our predecessor approved, confirmed, and blessed their Institute, as it was comprised within a certain norm of life drawn up by them in conformity with the truth of the Gospel and the sanctions of the holy Fathers, that thus the bond of charity and the unity might be preserved both among those companions themselves and among others who would desire to follow the same Institute.[52]

The Institute, the 'norm of life', is to preserve the bond of charity and the unity within the body. These values are to be preserved and fostered in spite of the missionary dispersal of the first generation (the challenge posed by geography) and the sequence of one generation of Jesuits after another (the challenge posed by history). The desired union is to exist, not only among those of the first, or any particular, generation, but also between

---

[51] See the treatment of the General Examen in chapter 2, especially the discussion of the experiments.
[52] Technically this extract is from the introduction to the Formula rather than from the Formula itself (*Formula of the Institute*, n. 2).

Jesuits of all generations, for as long as God wants the Society to exist.[53]

In part VIII of the *Constitutions* we read:

> On both sides, the chief bond to cement the union of the members among themselves and with their head is the love of God our Lord. For when the superior and the subjects are closely united to his Divine and Supreme Goodness, they will very easily be united among themselves, through that same love which will descend from the Divine Goodness and spread to all other persons, and particularly to the body of the Society. (VIII. 1. 8 [671])[54]

The *Constitutions* are shot through with this awareness of God's love pouring into the body of the Society and into each member. For the individual Jesuit the high point of this experience of God's love comes in part VII, which deals with the missioning of the members into Christ's vineyard. To be loved is to be sent; to be sent is to be loved. One way of reading the *Constitutions* is to see them as revolving around part VII, with everything that comes before it being preparatory to this missioning, and everything that follows as flowing from it. Parts VIII to X deal with the corporate supports for that missioning: union of minds and hearts, spiritual governance, and ways of going forward as a body into God's future.

Dominique Bertrand suggests that the process or movement articulated in the *Constitutions* is incarnational: the taking on of a body, the creation of a body to house and express the spirit that cries out to be enfleshed in a corporate way. The charism (which is spirit) needs a body (which is flesh and blood, inculturated and historical). Hence the *Constitutions* might be subtitled *Un corps pour l'Ésprit* or, with a somewhat different emphasis, *A Spirit in Search of a Body*.[55] This body is both individual (personal) and social (corporate). The spirit or charism must become enfleshed in the body (the total physico-spiritual personality) of each member.

---

[53] This interpretation may go beyond the exact meaning of the text.

[54] We will return to this key paragraph in chapter 5.

[55] Dominique Bertrand, *Un corps pour l'Ésprit: Essai sur l'expérience communautaire selon les Constitutions de la Compagnie de Jésus* (Paris: Desclée de Brouwer, 1974).

Then that same spirit or charism must become enfleshed in the body (the total physico-spiritual-social entity) of the Society. As the *Constitutions* unfold, the body (the individual) grows and develops, while at the same time, and *through* this development, becoming more and more integrated into the body (the social, corporate entity) that is the Society. This, in its turn, continues to grow and to manifest itself in a more and more elaborate way.

With typical Ignatian adaptability we should use whatever approach to the *Constitutions* helps us most, whatever key unlocks their treasure. As stimulus we might turn to Pedro Arrupe as he grapples with the complexity of the *Constitutions*[56] while encouraging Jesuits to ponder them and make of them a spiritual resource:

> Our spirit grasps the *Constitutions* as a book of norms, but at the same time as a book of life, not only because it is for life, but because in it there is latent a charism, a living gift of the Spirit who gives life, and who is the principle of unity and of action ... and [who] increases our capacity for growth and for the assimilation of the progress of humanity and of the Church. By means of a kind of interiorised metabolism, the charism which is latent in the *Constitutions* develops, adapts and strengthens the organism which is sustained by them—the Society of Jesus—in its continual 'coming-into-being' in history.[57]

[56] This complexity has always been a problem. Bobadilla wrote to Paul IV in the lead-up to the First General Congregation: 'The *Constitutions* and Declarations are a labyrinth altogether confused. They are so numerous that no one, either subject or superior, can come to know them, much less to observe them.' (MHSJ MN 4, 733)

[57] Pedro Arrupe, *A Planet to Heal* (Rome: International Centre for Jesuit Education, 1977), 273.

2.

DISCERNING AND NURTURING A VOCATION

IT IS DIFFICULT FOR US TODAY to realise how radical the Society of Jesus seemed in the mid-sixteenth century. Jesuits claimed to be religious,[1] yet they did not sing (or even recite) the Divine Office in common, nor have a regime of penances obligatory on all, nor wear a distinctive religious habit. Not only were these innovations seen as in discontinuity with the revered tradition of religious life reaching back to the Fathers of the Desert, but they could be interpreted as a surrender to some of the criticisms of the Protestant Reformers (and those of Christian humanists such as Erasmus). Then there was the Fourth Vow of special obedience to the Pope concerning missions, superfluous in the eyes of some (since the vow of obedience taken by all religious implicitly includes obedience to the Pope), arrogant in the eyes of others (as claiming a special relationship with the Vicar of Christ). Underlying all these new features was Ignatius' vision of a religious life that was radically decloistered, not only in comparison with monasticism but even with the life of the mendicant friars. There seemed to be a secular quality about this new order that was a scandal to traditionalists.[2]

---

[1] Nevertheless, they are cautious in the language they use. Note the comment of Joseph Conwell: 'They are not like anything seen before, and so they call themselves "societas", a *company* or *companionship*, a word not used of religious orders at that time, but of pious associations', in *Impelling Spirit: Revisiting a Founding Experience, 1539: Ignatius of Loyola and His Companions* (Chicago: Loyola, 1997), xxv–xxvi.

[2] The chief, but not the only, opponent of these innovations, and of Ignatian spirituality in general, was the Dominican theologian Melchor Cano. Polanco wrote of him: 'The conviction that both Ignatius and his companions were the precursors of the Antichrist began to take root in his heart and could not be eradicated. He wanted to make the signs of the Antichrist and his ministers apply perfectly to our men.' See *Year by Year with the Early Jesuits: Selections from the Chronicon of Juan de Polanco, S.J.*, translated and annotated by John Patrick Donnelly (St Louis: Institute of Jesuit Sources, 2004), 80. For a fuller discussion see Terence O'Reilly, 'Melchor Cano and the Spirituality of St Ignatius Loyola', in *Ignacio de Loyola y su tiempo*, edited by Juan Plazaolo (Bilbao: U. de Deusto, 1992), 369–380.

With historical hindsight one can argue that to push these innovations even a little further could have taken the Society of Jesus out of the category of a religious order and into the category (not formally recognised by the Church until the twentieth century) of a Secular Institute.[3] Such was the radical nature of Ignatius' original vision. When Hans Urs von Balthasar was faced with the decision either to remain a Jesuit, or to leave so as to devote himself to his collaboration with Adrienne von Speyr and to his involvement with the Community of St John (a Secular Institute), his reasoning is intriguing.

> In Basel, the mission of Adrienne von Speyr ... was decisive. What Ignatius had intended in his time meant henceforth for me 'secular institute'; the hard sacrifice demanded by this transition was accompanied by the certainty of serving the same idea more exactly.[4]

This rather dense statement seems to imply that von Balthasar saw the Secular Institute as the form that consecrated life, animated by the Ignatian spirit, would take (at least for him) in the twentieth century. He left the Jesuits with deep regret and pain, but with complete certainty that he was not abandoning any of the values and aspirations that Ignatius had conceived for the Society. It is only a small step to conclude that von Balthasar thought that, if Ignatius had been living in the twentieth century, he might well have founded a Secular Institute ('serving the same idea more exactly').

---

[3] On Secular Institutes see the *Code of Canon Law*, nn. 710–730, and commentary by Sharon L. Holland in *The Code of Canon Law: A Text and Commentary*, edited by James A. Coriden and others (New York and Mahwah: Paulist, 1985), 526–533. In recent times unease about the 'secularity' of the Society of Jesus was expressed by Paul VI in his observations on two documents produced by the 32nd General Congregation, the decree 'Our Mission Today: *Diaconia Fidei* and the Promotion of Justice' and the declaration 'Jesuits Today'. He refers to the Society as 'founded ... for a particularly spiritual and supernatural end' and continues, 'Every other undertaking should be subordinated to this end and carried out in a way appropriate for an Institute which is religious, not secular, and priestly' (*General Congregation 32*, appendix, in *Jesuit Life and Mission Today*, 398).
[4] Hans Urs von Balthasar, 'In Retrospect: 1965', in *My Work in Retrospect* (San Francisco: Ignatius, 1993), 89. For a discussion of von Balthasar's leaving the Society see Peter Henrici, 'Hans Urs von Balthasar: A Sketch of His Life', in *Hans Urs von Balthasar: His Life and Work*, edited by David L. Schindler (San Francisco: Ignatius, 1991), 19–23.

Whatever we may think of von Balthasar's argument, it helps us to understand why the early Jesuits had to spend so much time and energy in explaining who they were and how they differed from other orders. They frequently found themselves on the defensive. There was need for an ongoing *apologia*. We have only to think of the efforts of Nadal over many years to articulate the nature and spirit of the Society.[5] But even in the foundational documents themselves, such as the *Formula of the Institute* and the *Constitutions*, there are places where it seems clear that Ignatius is eager to emphasize and explain how the Society differs from the older orders, while taking their similarities for granted.[6]

The need to present the Society candidly and accurately arose first in relation to church authorities. Without their understanding and support there would have been no papal approbation of the order in 1540 and 1550. There was also a need to present the Society to the faithful, those people to whom the Society wished to minister (although not exclusively, since work among the 'infidel'—non-believers—was also part of its apostolic goal). The Society needed credibility in order to be apostolically effective. But a third category also existed, namely those who showed an interest in joining the Society. Candidates needed to know as fully as possible the nature of the body that they were seeking to join. Our focus in this chapter will be on a document that aims at meeting this special need (although this is only part of its purpose). It is usually known as the General Examen.

Genre of the Document

This title is actually a misnomer, due to a copyist's error in text D (1594).[7] The correct title for the whole document is quite simply Examen. This then is subdivided into the General Examen, which

---

[5] See Joseph F. Conwell, *Walking in the Spirit: A Reflection on Jerónimo Nadal's Phrase 'Contemplative Likewise in Action'* (St Louis: Institute of Jesuit Sources, 2003), also William V. Bangert, *Jerome Nadal, S.J., 1507–1580: Tracking the First Generation of Jesuits*, edited and completed by Thomas M. McCoog (Chicago: Loyola UP, 1992).

[6] The well-known statement 'What pertains to the vow of chastity requires no interpretation' (*Constitutions* VI. 1. 1 [547]) has to be understood in this context. The requirements of the vow of chastity are no different for Jesuits than for other religious. But those of obedience and poverty do differ. There is further discussion of this in chapter 3.

[7] See de Aldama, *Introductory Commentary*, 22–23.

constitutes the first four chapters, and the Particularised Examens, which constitute the remaining four. The first group of chapters is addressed to all applicants, while the last four chapters are addressed to different types of applicants: priests and those destined for ordination (chapter 5), those to be admitted as spiritual or temporal coadjutors (chapter 6), scholastics before and after their studies (chapter 7) and, finally, those admitted as indifferent, that is, those who enter with an openness to accept the grade for which they will show themselves most suitable.[8] I shall nevertheless continue to refer to the whole document as the General Examen in line with custom, and so as to distinguish it from the contemporary Consciousness (or Awareness) Examen, which is frequently referred to today simply as the Examen.[9]

The primary source of the document is the *Formula of the Institute* and its concern is twofold. The first is that a person should be made fully aware of what a commitment to the Society will involve. The second is a corollary to this, namely that no one will be admitted whose life (conduct or way of living) and doctrine (world-view or system of beliefs and values) have not been thoroughly examined. In other words, it is a document which enables the Society (a) to instruct the one who wants to enter, *so that he may know the Society*, and (b) to examine the one who wants to enter, *so that the Society may know him*. This combination of instruction and examination sets up a process or dynamic of mutual discernment.[10] Its purpose, but also the spirit in which it is to be conducted, is well articulated in the statement:

> The aim is that both sides may be content and satisfied while proceeding with greater clarity in everything, while all things

---

[8] For clarification on the nature and history of classes or 'grades' in the Society see L. Lukacs, 'De graduum diversitate inter sacerdotes in Societate Iesu', *AHSI*, 37 (1968), 237–316; Antonio M. de Aldama, 'De coadiutoribus Societatis Iesu in mente et in praxi S. Ignatii', *AHSI*, 38 (1969), 389–430.

[9] The seminal article in the modern rethinking of the daily examination of conscience is by George A. Aschenbrenner, 'Consciousness Examen', *Review for Religious*, 31 (1972), 14–21. Many others have followed.

[10] This process, specifically geared to the purpose of the General Examen, can also be seen as an introduction to 'our way of proceeding' over the years of formation and even beyond.

> are being directed and ordered toward greater service and
> praise of God our Lord (Examen 8.3[133]).

This sums up the elements necessary in any spiritual dialogue:
clarity, sincerity, indifference (in the Ignatian sense), so that,
whatever the outcome of the discernment (to enter or not to enter
the Society), God may be better served.

Uniqueness of the Document

The General Examen is a unique document in the history of
religious life. Monks, from early times, did not easily admit new
members to their monasteries. The Constitutions of the Dominican
Order prescribed that three competent friars be appointed in each
convent to examine candidates and to report to the prior and
chapter.[11] But none of these earlier traditions produced a book or
document to be used in such an examination. This uniqueness
of the General Examen means that we have nothing with which
to compare it or that might throw light on how to interpret it.
Where should we look for a key?

The key lies in the mind of Ignatius, in what we know from
elsewhere of his characteristic way of thinking. This is practical
rather than theoretical, inductive rather than deductive, existential
rather than essential, developmental rather than classical. This
mindset does not change from one situation to another or from
one text to another. It should not surprise us, therefore, if we
get most help in interpreting the General Examen from our
knowledge of the *Spiritual Exercises*. These give us the parallel we
need.

It is a commonplace that we cannot grasp the essential
character of the *Exercises* simply by a textual analysis. One has
to have the experience of making them oneself and (perhaps equally
important for understanding their dynamic) of accompanying
others who are making them. The text merely points to this
dynamic; it does not disclose it. Similarly with the General
Examen: a textual analysis leads to a very limited understanding
of the document and its purpose; it too merely points to a dynamic

---

[11] De Aldama, *Introductory Commentary*, 21–22. The author gives references to Pachomius,
Cassian and Benedict as well as to the Dominican Constitutions.

or a process. But, relying on the parallel with the *Exercises*, we may at least be able to offer some insight into what the General Examen involves. It will help if we can put ourselves imaginatively into the situation as described in the text. In what follows I am drawing on an enlightening article by Michael J. Buckley.[12] His summary statement can be our starting-point:

> The General Examen involved a process, very much like the Spiritual Exercises, conducted with the same care for withdrawal, direction, and discernment, lasting over a period of 'twelve to twenty days or longer if it seems good to the superior' [Examen 4.33 (90)], in which an applicant was able in solitude to sound out the depths or the solidity of his election to this way of life.[13]

This statement now needs to be unpacked with reference to the text of the General Examen itself. Note that this process is to take place somewhere separate from the house of novitiate. After stating that the candidate 'ought on several occasions to see and ponder the bulls of the Institute of the Society, and the *Constitutions* and rules which he must observe in it', we read:

> The first time is when he is in the house of the first probation, where those desiring to enter the Society are customarily received as guests for twelve or fifteen days so that they may reflect more carefully upon their whole situation, before they enter a house or college of the Society to live and associate with the others (Examen 1.13 [18]).

And again:

> ... at their first entrance the candidates are kept apart from the rest for twelve or fifteen days, or even as long as twenty, in the house of the first probation, as will be seen in Part I of the *Constitutions* (Examen 1.H[21]).

This refers forward to the paragraph beginning:

---

[12] Michael J. Buckley, 'Freedom, Election, and Self-Transcendence: Some Reflections upon the Ignatian Development of a Life of Ministry', in *Ignatian Spirituality in a Secular Age*, edited by George P. Schner (Waterloo, Ontario: Wilfrid Laurier UP, 1984), 65–90. Part 2, 74–80, is particularly relevant.
[13] Buckley, 'Freedom, Election, and Self-Transcendence', 75.

> We are strongly convinced in our Lord that it is of great importance for the service of his Divine and Supreme Majesty through this least Society that those received in it not only be tested for a long time before incorporation into it but also be well known before they are admitted to the probation which is made by living in common with those of the house [i.e. the novitiate probation]. Hence, it is good that next to where we live in common there be quarters where those being admitted may stay as guests .... (*Constitutions* I.4.1[190]).

The following Declaration adds:

> Where there cannot be a different house of first probation next to our own, some separation should be procured within the house so that those being received will have less occasion to converse with persons other than those appointed by the superior (I.4.A[191]).

I have quoted these texts at some length to show how sure Ignatius was about the setting he required for the process of the General Examen. This environment is remarkably similar to that deemed necessary for the Spiritual Exercises. We are reminded immediately of Annotation 20.[14] There is the same stress on withdrawal, on separation, on not socialising, on solitude.

> The purpose is that he may with greater freedom deliberate with himself and with God our Lord about his vocation and intention to serve his Divine and Supreme Majesty in this Society (I.4.4[197]).

The intention of Ignatius could hardly be clearer. He wants a person to experience the process of the General Examen in a location separate from the novitiate, in an atmosphere conducive to an undisturbed and prayerful examination of his vocation, in touch with his personal history and freedom. Ignatius is keen to avoid the effects of a premature socialisation with other Jesuits,

---

[14] 'Ordinarily, in making them an exercitant will achieve more progress the more he or she withdraws from all friends and acquaintances, and from all earthly concerns; for example, by moving out of one's place of residence and taking a different house or room where one can live in the greatest possible solitude.' (Exx 20)

even with novices, fearing the effects of a group dynamic on the individual's freedom to choose.[15]

Four-Part Structure

Besides the choosing of an appropriate location, the General Examen also resembles the Exercises in having a four-part structure. And within this structure, as with the Exercises, the process leads to a deepening of interiority and a sharpening of challenge. The first chapter deals with the Society itself, with particular emphasis on the ways in which it differs from the older orders. This stress is to disabuse the applicant of any misleading expectations he might have, arising from prior acquaintance with monastic or other already existing forms of religious life. More positively, it clarifies the nature of the Society as a thoroughly apostolic body. This is underlined by the special reference to the Fourth Vow of obedience to the Pope in the matter of missions (Examen 1. 5 [7]).[16] The second chapter explores whether there exist in the applicant's life or background any impediments to his entry into the Society.[17] If such exist, the General Examen immediately comes to an end. Otherwise the process continues.

So far the information exchanged by the Society's representative and the applicant has been mostly factual and dealing with externals.

---

[15] In spite of this, the practice of having a 'house of first probation' has been lost in the Society. This, in turn, has led to a watering down of the process of the General Examen. Buckley is trenchant in his critique of this development: '... the elimination of the house of first probation and the consequent absence of the steady appropriation of autobiographical religious experience which the process of the General Examen envisaged for those entering the Society, is a loss of capital importance'. He goes on to reflect on what he calls 'a number of correlative displacements'. See 'Freedom, Election, and Self-Transcendence', 78. Since Buckley's article appeared, the Common Norms promulgated by the 34th General Congregation (1995) have modified the requirements in the *Constitutions*. 'Those who seem suitable for the Society should spend some days of first probation ... inside or outside the community of the novices' (*Complementary Norms*, n. 31, in *The Constitutions of the Society of Jesus and Their Complementary Norms* [St Louis: Institute of Jesuit Sources, 1996]). The development of candidacy programmes in many provinces has also altered the way in which the first probation is envisaged.

[16] A fuller treatment of this Fourth Vow is given in part VII (*Constitutions* VII. 1. 1–8 [603–617]). See chapter 4.

[17] Many of these impediments come from the general Canon Law of the Church; some relate more explicitly to life in the Society. The latter focus on the applicant's inner stability, and with an eye to a life of ministry, on his public credibility.

In chapter 3 the questioning of the candidate becomes more personal, more autobiographical. It demands of him an ability to articulate his religious experience, as well as great trust in revealing himself intimately. He is asked about the pattern of prayer in his life, and about those personal experiences of God that have fostered an affective relationship with him. This deep sharing by the applicant makes him better known to the Society (in the person of the Jesuit 'giving' the General Examen), but it also reveals the applicant to himself in a clearer way than heretofore. Again we recognise some of the dynamics of the Exercises, and indeed of any good spiritual direction. Without such self-knowledge the applicant would be less able to continue discerning his call to the Society of Jesus

At this point the force and depth of the questioning becomes quite startling.

> Is he determined to abandon the world and to follow the counsels of Christ our Lord?
>
> How much time has elapsed since he made this general decision to abandon the world?
>
> After making this decision, has he wavered in it, and to what extent? About how much time has elapsed since his desires to leave the world and follow the counsels of Christ our Lord began to come? What were the signs or motives through which they came? (Examen 3.13[50])

Let us remind ourselves that these questions are addressed to a person who has not yet been admitted to the novitiate! Note the strength of the word 'determined' and the starkness of the phrase 'to abandon the world and to follow the counsels of Christ our Lord', a phrase that is repeated so as to underline its seriousness.[18] There is a presupposition that the fundamental desires or attraction have been to the religious life as such (hence the wording 'general decision').[19] The history of these desires is thoroughly investigated. How much time has elapsed, has he

---

[18] The language echoes that found in the offering at the end of the exercise on the Call of the King: 'I wish and desire, and it is my deliberate decision ...' (Exx 98).
[19] Leaving the world and following the evangelical counsels was the traditional way of referring to entering religious life.

wavered, what were the signs and motives that conveyed or mediated these desires? The whole development of his discernment and the subsequent determination to enter religious life is teased out, so as to be clarified, better understood and personally appropriated.[20]

Then the questioning continues:

> Does he have a deliberate determination in the Lord to live and die with and in this Society of Jesus our Creator and Lord? And since when? Where and through whom was he first moved to this? (Examen 3.14[51])

The process of the questioning is similar, only now it focuses on the candidate's desires in relation to the Society. Is this the particular religious order to which he is being called? Once again there is the issue of determination—not a determination to enter the novitiate, but 'to live and die with and in this Society of Jesus'. A tentative, provisional, weak desire is not enough. Then, having probed the depth of the applicant's desire and challenged his determination, the General Examen draws out the history of such a desire and resolve. The applicant is being asked to revisit a crucial dimension of his autobiography: how God led him from the time when he first noticed an attraction to the Society. It is like Ignatius himself being requested by Nadal 'to tell us how the Lord had guided him from the beginning of his conversion'.[21]

We might notice also that Ignatius does not inquire about the applicant's attitude towards living and dying 'in' the Society, but living and dying 'with and in' this Society of Jesus. The phrase 'with and in' has the effect of further personalising the question and underlining the dimension of relationships. The Society is not simply an organization to which a Jesuit belongs,

---

[20] Ignatius brings his views on 'determination' to a logical, though very harsh, conclusion in the *Directory Dictated to Juan Alonso de Vitoria*, 'There have been persons who took the path of religious life and did not persevere in it but refused to bend to the sweet yoke of the Lord, and have consequently gone to hell because they abandoned religious life and through their own fault died apostate' (*On Giving the Spiritual Exercises: The Early Jesuit Manuscript Directories and the Official Directory of 1599*, translated and edited by Martin E. Palmer [St Louis: Institute of Jesuit Sources, 1996], 21).

[21] Tylenda, *Pilgrim's Journey*, 123.

but a companionship, a network of 'friends in the Lord' with whom a person lives and follows Christ in love, on mission, until death. The relationship with God in Christ is intimately connected with, and mediated by, the relationship that the applicant fosters with other Jesuits.[22]

Commentators on the General Examen rightly emphasize Ignatius' insistence on an applicant's having a resolute determination, even before being admitted to the novitiate, to live the Jesuit life until death. We might more readily expect such a determination at first vows (end of the novitiate) and even more so at final vows. Ignatius' expectations of the applicant seem excessively high, perhaps overly idealistic. But we know from elsewhere that part of Ignatius' pedagogy was to lay out, as far as possible, all the demands of a process at its very inception. In the Exercises an enormous challenge is put to the retreatant before they even begin.

> The persons who make the Exercises will benefit greatly by entering upon them with great spirit and generosity toward their Creator and Lord, and by offering all their desires and freedom to him so that His Divine Majesty can make use of their persons and of all they possess in whatsoever way is in accord with his most holy will (Exx 5).

This annotation anticipates the *Suscipe* prayer in the Contemplation to Attain Love at the end of the Exercises (Exx 234). Ignatius always looks for great desires, magnanimity and resolve, and trusts that in the ensuing process (whether that of the Exercises or of Jesuit life) these will take even deeper root and become ever greater.

A Problem Explored

What commentators tend to gloss over is Ignatius' assumption that an applicant to join the Society will have previously 'determined to abandon the world and to follow the counsels of Christ our

---

[22] The phrase, although inverted, occurs again in one of the Particularised Examens dealing with the coadjutors: 'From then on they remain as formed coadjutors, either spiritual or temporal, in such a way that on their side they are perpetually obliged to live and die in our Lord in and with this Society' (Examen 6.8[119]).

Lord' (Examen 3.13 [50]). As we have seen, he probes this matter in depth and seeks to uncover the history of this determination. In other words, he presumes that the applicant first discovers his vocation to religious life as such, and only then is led by the Lord to focus his intention on the Society. There are several difficulties with such an assumption.

This pattern does not correspond with many Jesuits' experience of call. Some may well have travelled by this route but others never considered entering any order other than the Society. From the beginning their focus was on becoming a Jesuit. If the Society refused to accept them they would take up the responsibilities of the lay Christian life or become a secular priest. Ignatius, by contrast, seems to expect that a person who is turned away by the Society will enter another religious order to carry out his initial determination. He cannot imagine someone who has been so determined turning back again to 'the world'. If he is not suited to the Society he will find some other order that will accept him. Is there a hint of condescension here?

However, a more benign interpretation of Ignatius' assumption simply acknowledges the important differences between the Society and other forms of religious life. The Society's total commitment to mission (lived out through active ministry) cannot be subsumed into the same category as, for example, the monastic life. God's call or vocation is always specific to one particular form of religious life, not to religious life in general. Perhaps, given the extraordinary fascination with prayer and mysticism in Ignatius' time (especially in Spain and Portugal), he foresaw candidates seeking admission to the Society wanting to give long hours to prayer.[23] Such people would be unsuitable for (and

---

[23] Even some who were already members of the Society sought long hours of prayer. The most dramatic examples were Fr Andrea de Oviedo and the scholastic Francisco Onfroy. In 1548 Ignatius had tried to deal with this issue by commissioning Polanco to send a long letter on obedience to Oviedo (Ignatius, *Letters*, 237–245). The following year he commissioned his secretary to send an even longer letter to Francis Borgia with a detailed critique of Oviedo's and Onfroy's position on the necessity of long periods of prayer. It also contains a repudiation of Onfroy's views on the reform of the Church and the Society (Ignatius, *Letters*, 266–283). Borgia himself had an ingrained tendency towards lengthy prayer and Ignatius (in between the two letters above) wrote to him in strong terms advising him toward moderation (Ignatius, *Letters*, 253–256). See also

unhappy in) the Society, but they might well have a vocation to an eremitical or monastic way of life. This interpretation may help to justify in part Ignatius' assumption but it does not make it universal.

Another difficulty with Ignatius' assumption is that it does not allow for the fact that many have sought entry into the Society in order, primarily, to become priests.[24] They experience this as their fundamental vocation, qualified of course by a realisation that their priesthood is to be lived out 'with and in' the Society of Jesus. But being a priest has a higher priority for them than being a religious. Priesthood is their primary identity. Religious life is the context of their priesthood, offering them the support that comes from belonging to a faith community. Or as the first priest-companions said in the Deliberation, giving an explicitly apostolic reason for forming themselves into one body:

> Everyone should have concern for and comprehension of the others for greater apostolic efficacy, since united strength would have more power and courage in confronting whatever challenging goals were to be sought than if this strength were divided into many parts (*Deliberation*, n.3).

Candidates with such desires around priesthood, if the Society refuses to accept them, are more likely to become secular priests (or remain in lay life) than join another religious order.

M. Ruiz Jurado, 'Un caso de profetismo reformista en la Compañía de Jésus: Gandia 1547–1549', *AHSI*, 43 (1974), 217–266.

[24] A developing theology of priesthood (and of Church) means that the desire to become an ordained priest has varied nuances in different periods of history, and even in different geographical locations. Currently there is a lack of a clear consensus on the nature of Jesuit priesthood in spite of decree 6 of the 34th Jesuit General Congregation, entitled 'The Jesuit Priest: Ministerial Priesthood and Jesuit Identity'. Helpful resources include Luis de Diego, *La opción sacerdotal de Ignacio de Loyola y sus compañeros, 1515–1540* (Caracas: Centrum Ignatianum UCAB, 1975); Michael J. Buckley, 'Jesuit Priesthood: Its Meaning and Commitments', *Studies in the Spirituality of Jesuits*, 8/5 (1976); Michael J. Buckley, '"Likewise You Are Priests … "': Some Reflections on Jesuit Priesthood', in *Spirit, Style, Story: Essays Honoring John W. Padberg*, edited by Thomas M. Lucas (Chicago: Loyola, 2002), 3–31; William J. Harmless and Donald L. Gelpi, 'Priesthood Today and the Jesuit Vocation', *Studies in the Spirituality of Jesuits*, 19/3 (1987); and for the wider historical background, John W. O'Malley, 'Priesthood, Ministry, and Religious Life: Some Historical and Historiographical Considerations', *Theological Studies*, 49 (1988), 223–257, reprinted in O'Malley, *Tradition and Transition: Historical Perspectives on Vatican II* (Wilmington: Michael Glazier, 1989), 127–171.

Furthermore, as with the specific attraction to priesthood, many candidates have been drawn to the Society specifically for the apostolic opportunities it offers. They experience an inner imperative to evangelize: to preach, teach and heal. Religious life and priesthood are both seen as means to this end, the context in which evangelization is lived out. These candidates are choosing the apostolate first and its mode and context second. They too, if turned down by the Society, are not going to join another religious order because of a prior determination to 'leave the world and follow the counsels of Christ our Lord', although they might join one if it seems to offer equal or greater apostolic opportunities. This may well be the mentality of young adults in today's Western world who are drawn to consider the Society. It is also significant how many Jesuits who have left the Society in recent decades continue in the same or similar ministries to those they exercised as Jesuits. Indeed some have left precisely because they felt inhibited rather than helped by the Society in engaging in certain ministries.

We often look for parallels between requirements in the General Examen and *Constitutions*, and the pattern of Ignatius' own life. But, in examining what we have been calling his 'assumption' in Examen 3.13–14[50–51], we find that no parallel exists, rather the opposite. We might say that the General Examen transposes the order of desires. It expects to hear of a generic attraction and commitment to religious life first, then later 'a deliberate determination in the Lord to live and die with and in this Society'. There is no explicit mention of priesthood at this point. But Ignatius, having left aside the issue of religious life very soon after his initial conversion,[25] was led first to want a life devoted to the apostolate *(aiudar a las almas)*, then to priesthood as a way of carrying out that desire, and finally, as an unforeseen step, to become a religious. Even then, he and the First Companions had to create a radically new kind of religious life in the Church, unlike anything that had gone before. Nothing was allowed or required in this religious life that might dilute or

---

[25] Ignatius was no more than toying with the idea of religious life at this point (*Autobiography*, n.12). He had not yet learned fully how to discern.

hamper in any way its aim and purpose: mission. Perhaps the kind of person described in the previous paragraph is closest to the development of Ignatius himself.

A Magisterial Text

By the end of chapter 3 of the General Examen, the Society should be satisfied with the applicant's determination and convinced that his resolve has been the result of a free and well-informed election. Continuing the comparison with the Exercises, Buckley describes the transition into the final part of the process:

> In the Exercises, the election is followed by the Third and Fourth Week, the cost and glory of discipleship; in the General Examen, this confirmation that an election has been made is followed by one of the most profound descriptions of this cost ever written by Ignatius, the great fourth chapter of the General Examen. In both the Exercises and the Examen, this is the moment in which the disciple hears and lives with the words, 'If anyone will come after me ....'[26]

Much of the teaching in this chapter can be gathered under the heading of 'renunciation'. It moves from the renunciation of temporal goods (Examen 4.1–5 [53–59]), through the renunciation of family ties (Examen 4.6–C [60–62]), to the renunciation of self (Examen 4.8–33 [63–90]). It begins with what is external and impersonal, then moves to the intimate area of personal relationships, and ends with the most difficult renunciation of all, that of the self. This rubric of renunciation places Ignatius in continuity with the oldest tradition of religious life, that of the desert (even though in other ways he was turning that tradition upside down).[27] Ignatius had learnt much about renunciation in

---

[26] Buckley, 'Freedom, Election, and Self-Transcendence', 77–78.
[27] 'The first step in monastic life is *apotage*, or *apotaxis*, renunciation. The monk must renounce not only evil and Satan, but some good aspects of life as well, summarised in family and riches, what is called *cosmos*, the world. The world, though good, is a source of care and of division. Renunciation, therefore, invites to embracing both chastity and poverty. The purpose is to be *amerimnos*, without care in the world (1 Corinthians 7:32–35), to be wholly available for the service of God.' (Joseph F. Conwell, *Impelling Spirit: Revisiting a Founding Experience: 1539 Ignatius of Loyola and His Companions* [Chicago:

the years following his conversion. In his own development he had abandoned the excesses of his stay at Manresa in line with his changing motivation. Yet he knew that renunciation was central to Christian living and now he wants the candidate 'to seek in our Lord his greater abnegation and continual mortification in all things possible' (Examen 4.46[103]). But the stress is more on interior mortification or abnegation, a renunciation that becomes ever more spiritual. Its purpose is the inner freedom of the apostle to give himself totally to mission.

Such inner freedom is not cheaply won. But the struggle to attain it, the renunciations that are necessary, must be placed in a contemplative context. They need to become an expression of the desire for union with the poor and suffering Christ. So, having spelt out the means to reaching this freedom, Ignatius ends his ascetical exposition with a passage of, for him, unusual lyricism:

> They desire to clothe themselves with the same garb and uniform of their Lord because of the love and reverence owed to him, to such an extent that where there would be no offence to his Divine Majesty and no imputation of sin to the neighbour, they desire to suffer injuries, false accusations, and affronts, and to be held and esteemed as fools (but without their giving any occasion for this), because of their desire to resemble and imitate in some manner our Creator and Lord Jesus Christ, by putting on his garb and uniform, since it was for our spiritual profit that he clothed himself as he did. For he gave us an example that in all things possible to us we might seek, with the aid of his grace, to imitate and follow him, since he is the way which leads men to life. Therefore, the candidate should be asked whether he finds himself with such desires, which are so salutary and fruitful for the perfection of his soul. (Examen 4.44[101])

The question now put to the applicant is not about determination but about desires. This is a significant shift of emphasis. Ignatius has here opened up part of his soul, and he

Loyola, 1997], 231) Readers may be more conversant with the Latin terms *fuga mundi* and *contemptus mundi*.

knows from his own experience that what he is seeking in the applicant can only be *de arriba,* that is, pure gift from God. With this in mind, and conscious of the demands of this grace, he continues:

> Where through human weakness and personal misery the candidate does not experience in himself such ardent desires in our Lord, he should be asked whether he has any desires to experience them. If he answers affirmatively that he does wish to have such holy desires, then, so that he may the better reach them in fact, he should be questioned further ....
> (Examen 4.45 [102])

In all this there is a striking parallel with his teaching on the Third Way of Being Humble in the *Spiritual Exercises.* Indeed, it can be argued that both texts describe the same grace.

> The Third Way of Being Humble is the most perfect, and consists in this. When I possess the first and second ways, and when the options equally further the praise and glory of God, in order to imitate Christ Our Lord better and to be more like him here and now, I desire and choose poverty with Christ poor rather than wealth; contempt with Christ laden with it rather than honours. Even further, I desire to be regarded as a useless fool for Christ, who before me was regarded as such, rather than as a wise and prudent person in this world. (Exx 167)

Does the applicant experience this desire? If not, does he at least experience a desire to have this desire?

At this point it may be well to recapitulate. We have been exploring a process of examination, taking place in an atmosphere of solitude, in which the Society reveals itself to the candidate and the candidate to the Society. This is followed by an even deeper investigation of the personal religious autobiography of the candidate, facilitated by the skilful questioning and listening of the examiner. This investigation, and the candidate's gradual articulation of his religious experience, enable him to own that experience more, to appropriate it as uniquely his own, and so to grow in freedom. Further focusing this process, the candidate is led through that part of his story since he first experienced desires to enter religious life and determined to do so, and then through that part of his story since this determination was first specified in terms of the Society of Jesus. He is then exposed, in the fourth chapter of the General Examen, to what Benedict, in the 58th chapter of his Rule, called the *dura et aspera* of religious life.[28] These are the traditional renunciations which are now reinterpreted by Ignatius in the light of the apostolic lifestyle of Jesuits. Finally the candidate is asked if he has an ardent desire to follow the poor and suffering Christ. If he answers in the affirmative, and if the examiner is satisfied, the candidate may be admitted into the novitiate.

Models of a Novitiate

There are two possible models of a novitiate. One operates on the understanding that novices are received so that over the period of novitiate they may discern whether or not they have a vocation to this particular form of religious life. This is the central issue for both the novice and the novice director. The novitiate, in other words, is a time for discernment, for making an election. If the novitiate is Ignatian, it will include the making of the Spiritual Exercises, and the main purpose of these Exercises will be to reach a decision, an election, on the issue of vocation.

The alternative model is built on very different presuppositions. These are that an election has already been made, and that the candidate on entering is already determined 'to live and die with and in this Society of Jesus'. The purpose of the novitiate is to seek ongoing confirmation of the election that has been made, to socialise the novice in the community that is the universal body of the Society, and to initiate his apprenticeship to ministry. When the Spiritual Exercises are made they will be geared to some goal other than the making of an election.[29]

It is clear that Ignatius is thinking of this second model in the General Examen and *Constitutions*. Even allowing for the ever-present flexibility in Ignatius' legislation, his willingness to adapt

---

[28] 'They should be exposed to all the trials of monastic life which appear to be hard and harsh but which lead us on our way to God.' (*Saint Benedict's Rule*, translation and introduction by Patrick Barry [Mahwah: HiddenSpring, 2004], 131)
[29] This statement will be elaborated on below.

to 'circumstances of persons, times, and places', it is difficult to defend the first model in properly Ignatian terms.

Innovation: Experiments and Experiences

There is widespread agreement that the pattern of formation in the Society not only grew out of, but is meant to be a re-enactment of, the experience of Ignatius and the early companions. This is not apparent from part III of the *Constitutions*, which deals with the novitiate. Here the influence of Polanco, and through him that of the rules and constitutions of other orders, is too pervasive. But the pattern is very clear in the General Examen, which expresses better the originality of Ignatius' own insights. This leads us to an examination of the six 'experiments' or experiences[30] that are proposed for novices in the General Examen: the Spiritual Exercises, ministry in hospitals, pilgrimage, humble service in the novitiate house, the teaching of catechism to children and the illiterate, and the priestly ministries of preaching and hearing confessions.[31] These experiments are built on the activities in which the First Companions engaged from their coming together in Paris until their residence in Rome.

Before we begin our own reflections it will be helpful to quote a passage penned by Ignatius in 1541 as a preliminary document to the writing of the *Constitutions*. He is aware that he is breaking new ground with the experiments and reflects on his motivation for doing so.

> The reason which impels us to give greater importance to experiments and to devote more time to them than is customarily employed in other congregations is the following: if someone enters a well-ordered and well-organised monastery, he will be more separated from occasions of sin because of the cloister, tranquillity and good order there than he will

[30] The Spanish word *experiencia* has three overlapping meanings: a) a testing or a trial, b) experience, in the sense of knowledge gained through doing rather than study, c) an experiment or placement through which such knowledge is gained.

[31] Note that in the General Examen the Exercises are considered as one of the experiments. Our contemporary usage tends to speak of the Exercises *and* the experiments, for example: 'John finished the Exercises around mid-February and began his first experiment in March'. This can be quite misleading.

be in our Society. For this Society does not have that cloister, quiet and repose, but travels from one place to another. Moreover, if one has bad habits and lacks some perfection, it suffices for him to perfect himself in a monastery so ordered and organised. But in our Society, it is necessary that one be well experienced and extensively tested before being admitted. For as he travels about later on, he must associate with men and women both good and bad. Such associations require greater strength and greater experiences, as well as greater graces and gifts from our Creator and Lord.[32]

This text offers us a 'composition of place', an imaginative yet concrete description of where the Society lives its life. Its members are called 'to help souls', and this will entail being wherever people are to be found. Hence the need to be frequently on the roads and on the high seas (and, in today's world, in the air). Against this background we can look first at the overall dynamic of the six experiments, and then say something more about each separately.

Joseph Veale expresses the dynamic as follows:

There are three stages, inseparable and interdependent, of entering into a spiritual appropriation of the Jesuit vocation. First, making the Exercises. Secondly, doing what St Ignatius called the experiences or experiments. Thirdly, returning from these two experiences to the text of the *Constitutions*.[33]

The interrelationships within this schema, this triad of Exercises, experiments and *Constitutions*, repay examination. The foundation of the schema, that without which nothing else happens, is the experience of the Exercises. The *Constitutions*, the third constituent of the schema, presuppose a person who, through the Exercises, knows experientially that he is loved by God; has to some degree attained indifference; realises that he is a forgiven sinner; has been grasped by the attractiveness and the ideals of

---

[32] MHSJ Const. 1, 60.
[33] Joseph Veale, 'How the *Constitutions* Work', in *Manifold Gifts: Ignatian Essays on Spirituality* (Oxford: Way Books, 2006), 79–98, here 84. See also, in the same volume, 'From Exercises to *Constitutions*: A Spirit in Search of a Body', 99–108.

Christ and has responded to his call; has learnt the art of discernment, especially from having been guided through such a process; knows what it is to suffer with Christ suffering and to rejoice in the joy of the Risen Christ; is sensitive to God's presence in all of creation, including his own life; and has emerged into the freedom of the Spirit.

But how can one be sure that these graces have been received and integrated during the Exercises? How does one find confirmation? By exposing the person, through the further experiments, to the tangible, messy, often painful existence of other people. The novice is invited to find God in the heart of this reality just as he found God in the seclusion and solitude of the Exercises. The interplay of the contrasting kinds of experience is vital; they form part of the one process. In a real sense the Exercises do not end with the thirty days, but are continued, and often brought alive in new and deeper ways, through the person's insertion into, and involvement with, the lives of the people to whom he is sent. The novice's indifference is now being tested; his sinfulness and dependence on God's mercy are experienced in fresh and possibly surprising ways; Christ is shedding light on complex human situations; the dying and rising of Christ is entered into through accompanying the dying and rising of his people; the need for discernment and for the unction of the Spirit is everywhere present. Confirmation will be recognised when this apprenticeship to apostolic ministry brings him inner peace and joy, the signs that his will and God's are in harmony.

Sequence of Experiences

The First Experience

Let us now reflect on each of the experiences or experiments individually. At first sight it would seem that the experiment needing least comment is the making of the Exercises. It is not only the first chronologically but the first in importance, a true 'principle and foundation' for the other five. Yet when we read the relevant texts in the General Examen and in part III they give rise to surprise and puzzlement. First the General Examen:

> The first experience consists in making the Spiritual Exercises for one month, a little more or less; that is to say, in the person's examining his conscience, thinking over his whole past life and making a general confession, meditating upon his sins, contemplating the events and mysteries of the life, death, resurrection, and ascension of Christ our Lord, exercising himself in praying vocally and mentally, according to the capacity of the persons, as he will be instructed in our Lord, and so on (Examen 4.10[65]).

If we consider the Spiritual Exercises outside the particular circumstances of the novitiate this paragraph cannot be said adequately to describe their dynamic, or even their purpose as it is presented in the text itself (Exx 1, 21). The Election, which most commentators today see as central to their dynamic, is conspicuously absent. But perhaps it will be mentioned in part III:

> Likewise, care should be taken both that they learn what is proper and not let it be forgotten, and that they put what they have learned into practice, all of them devoting time to spiritual things and striving to acquire devotion to the extent that divine grace imparts it to them. Toward this purpose, it will be helpful to give all or some of the Spiritual Exercises to those who have not made them, as may be judged expedient for them in our Lord. (*Constitutions* III.1.20[277])

Again there is no allusion to an election. The purpose of making the Exercises is the acquiring of devotion. All this would be quite incomprehensible if the novice were not assumed to have made his election before being admitted to the novitiate. But with this assumption it makes perfect sense.

The Spanish word *devoción* is problematic. The English equivalent fails to convey all that Ignatius implied by its use. For him devotion is not a vague sentiment or a warm feeling, still less anything that we might name as sentimentality. It is the experience of finding God.[34] In the *Autobiography* he describes the maturing of his own religious experience with precisely this term:

---

[34] Buckley helpfully links devotion with discernment in 'Freedom, Election, and Self-Transcendence', 81–82. See also his article, '*Semper crescendo in devotione ...* : Jesuit Spirituality as Stimulus to Ecumenism', *CIS*, 60 (1989), 63–101.

> He made a solemn avowal … that his devotion, that is, his ease in finding God, was always increasing, now more than ever in his entire life. At whatever time or hour he wanted to find God, he found him. (n. 99)

This was the gift desired by Ignatius for the novice, a gift to which he would be receptive through the making of the Exercises. Without this gift, without a facility in finding God, the other experiments would not produce their fruit which, in essence, would be the same fruit! If a novice did not find God in making the Exercises he was unlikely to find God in the hospitals or on the roads of Europe. And if he did not find God in the hospitals or on the roads of Europe he would not be suited for lifelong ministry in the Society of Jesus. The gift that is devotion is indispensable for Jesuit life.

The Second Experience

> The second experience is to serve for another month in hospitals or one of them. The candidates take their meals and sleep in it or in them, or serve for one or several hours during the day, according to the times, places, and persons. They should help and serve all, the sick and the well, in conformity with the directions they receive, in order to lower and humble themselves more, thus giving clear proof of themselves to the effect that they are completely giving up the world with its pomps and vanities, so that in everything they may serve their Creator and Lord, crucified for them. (Examen 4. 11 [66])

Sixteenth-century hospitals bore little resemblance to our technologically sophisticated and antiseptic institutions. They tended to cater mostly for society's outcasts, especially plague victims and those afflicted with syphilis. Many of these people had been abandoned by their families and friends. They were, to apply Nadal's phrase, those for whom nobody cared.[35]

Ignatius sent the novices into these hospitals partly because it was what he and his early companions had done, for example, during their months in the towns of northern Italy in 1537. A

---

[35] 'The Society has the care of those souls for whom either there is nobody to care or, if somebody ought to care, the care is negligent.' (*Orationis observationes*, MHSJ MN 6, 126)

first-hand account by Rodrigues gives us a sense of what such ministry involved. He is describing the arrival of the companions in Venice (1537) to join Ignatius, who was already there. They made certain decisions as to how to proceed, including one to work in hospitals.

> They therefore chose two hospitals in which to work with their poor and sick (one called Sts John and Paul and the other the Incurables), divided into two groups. Sometimes Ignatius, who was living in another house, visited them at work, and sometimes they visited him. In the hospitals they waited on the indigent, made the beds, swept the house, cleaned out whatever was soiled, washed the pots of the poor who were sick, carried away the bodies of the dead honourably prepared for burial, dug their graves and buried them in a religious manner. Day and night they were present to everyone with such care, fervour, joy and happiness that all those living in the hospitals were greatly astounded.[36]

Placed in similar circumstances, novices needed to embody in their lives the *kenosis* of Christ, through obedience, charity and humiliations. Christ had already emptied himself to become one with the lowliest of humanity. They in turn were to do what Christ had already done, to empty themselves of their natural clinging to honour and prestige in society, to leave aside even their natural sense of modesty and decency as they related to people whose sickness often carried a severe moral stigma.[37] They were to find the poor Christ in these people just as they had found him in the contemplations of his life when making the Exercises. They were to be the compassionate, healing Christ ministering to the broken, dying Christ. As well as a severe test, the hospital experiment was an effectual apprenticeship to Jesuit ministry.[38]

---

[36] *A Brief and Exact Account: The Recollections of Simão Rodrigues on the Origin and Progress of the Society of Jesus,* with translation, introduction and commentary by Joseph F. Conwell (St Louis: Institute of Jesuit Sources, 2004), 45–46.

[37] The closest contemporary parallel would be to work with victims of AIDS in a developing country.

[38] An interesting use of this experiment appears in the paragraph that deals with those who have left without permission but later return: 'When there is doubt about the constancy of those who return of their own accord, they could be placed in a hospital or

The Third Experience

The third experience has a twofold purpose, as the text of the General Examen makes clear:

> The third experience is to spend another month in making a pilgrimage without money, but begging from door to door at times, for the love of God our Lord, in order to grow accustomed to discomfort in food and lodging. Thus too the candidate, through abandoning all the reliance which he could have in money or other created things, may with genuine faith and intense love place his reliance entirely in his Creator and Lord. (Examen 4.12[67])

We might regard the first aim as ascetical and the second as contemplative or 'mystical'. There is no doubt that Ignatius regarded a capacity for physical endurance as necessary for a Jesuit, a requirement associated particularly with the matter of travel. Jesuits could expect to be constantly on the move which, in the sixteenth century, was uncomfortable and hazardous. He had earlier written, 'It seems that one who does not know how to remain and walk for a day without eating, and sleeping poorly because of this, could not persevere in the Society'.[39] The asceticism that was being tested was not an end in itself but was instrumental to the ministry of the future Jesuit.

But it was the second aim that was more important. The pilgrimage, undertaken without money or other natural resources, was to expose the novice to an insecurity in which he would place his reliance and confidence in God alone. Ignatius wanted his novice to hand himself over into God's care, leaving aside fear, and not (as we might say today) trying to take out insurance. This God is a God of relationship, a God of the covenant, who will not and cannot let us down. The pilgrimage was to be an experience of both actual and spiritual poverty.

Furthermore, like ministry in hospitals, the pilgrimage was an apprenticeship in the art of dealing with people. The novice had to form relationships with every kind of person whom God

---

in other experiences where, by serving Christ's poor out of love to him for some time, they may show their stability and constancy, and in part do penance for their earlier fickleness' (*Constitutions* II.3.D[240]).
[39] MHSJ Const. 1, 54.

placed in his path. These people were unknown, a cross-section of the population, sinners as well as saints, a random sample of that human race for whom Christ died. The novice must adjust, must again put aside his likes and dislikes, his pride and prejudice, his squeamishness and fastidiousness. He must meet life in the raw and find God amid its often harsh realities.[40]

The Fourth Experience

The next experience, located in the novitiate house, leaves behind the adventure and drama of the hospitals and the roads.

> The fourth experience consists in the candidate's employing himself, after entrance into the house, with all diligence and care in various low and humble offices, while giving a good example of himself in all of them (Examen 4.13[68]).

The very lowliness and even triviality of the tasks to be performed within one's own local community, the monotonous daily routine of duties, can often test obedience, charity and generosity more than apostolic enterprises. To serve our brothers can be harder than to serve the poor or the outcast. It is less likely to bring much gratification, still less excitement or matter for self-congratulation. One is reminded of the question put to the candidate at the end of chapter 4 of the General Examen:

> Is he determined and ready to accept and suffer with patience, with the help of God's grace, any such injuries, mockeries, and affronts entailed by the wearing of this uniform of Christ our Lord, and any other affronts offered him, whether by someone inside the house or the Society (where he desires to obey, abase himself, and gain eternal life) or outside it by any persons whatsoever on earth, returning them not evil for evil but good for evil? (Examen 4.45[102])

Neither the house nor the Society itself is seen as a safe haven from painful and humiliating confrontations.

---

[40] The practice of going on pilgrimage was deeply embedded in the Christian tradition. Even in parts of the monastic tradition, especially in its Celtic form, *peregrinatio* was highly esteemed. The emphasis was not on the place to which a person travels but on the actual journey itself. This was also the approach of Ignatius, but he innovates by making pilgrimage a means of formation for ministry.

Buckley has suggested that a parallel exists between the nature and use of this experiment and the practice of repetition in the Spiritual Exercises.[41] In an ordinary day within the Exercises there will be two contemplations, followed by repetitions. The latter are periods during which prayer takes on a greater simplicity, exercitants deepen and confirm what was experienced in the original contemplations, and are enabled to come to terms with anything that they could not face the first time around. Similarly the two experiments of hospital and pilgrimage are followed by this one. It is a repetition in a quieter, less dramatic, more familiar context (the Jesuit house) of the earlier experiences. In this way a deepening of experience is built into the sequence and structure of the experiments in just the way that it is built into the Spiritual Exercises.

The Fifth and Sixth Experiences

A notable change of emphasis appears in the fifth and sixth experiences. There is no longer any mention of an ascetical purpose, or even of the spiritual growth of the novice. The focus is simply on ministering to the needs of people. In other words, the apprenticeship model now dominates.

> The fifth experience is that of explaining the Christian doctrine or a part of it in public to boys and other simple persons, or of teaching it to individuals, as opportunity offers and what seems in our Lord more profitable and suitable to the persons (Examen 4.14[69]).

Yet, having acknowledged the explicitly apostolic nature of this experiment, there is no doubt that it does in practice call for abnegation and humility. This is particularly so if the novice is already an ordained priest, or a university graduate, or has come from an aristocratic background. We cannot doubt that Ignatius had this ascetical aspect in mind, not only here in the fifth experiment, but also in inserting the specific promise into the formula of profession that the Jesuit will have 'special care for the instruction of children' (*Constitutions* V.3.3[527], V.3.6[532], V.4.2[535]). We know that Ignatius insisted on this kind of activity

---

[41] Buckley, 'Freedom, Election, and Self-Transcendence', 83–84.

even for Laínez, Salmerón and Jay when he sent them, at the order of Paul III, to the Council of Trent.[42] For Ignatius, humble tasks fit well with those who hold high positions!

Finally we come to the sixth experiment, which of its nature is open only to the ordained.

> In a sixth experience the candidate, who has now been tested and found edifying, will proceed farther by preaching or hearing confessions, or in both together, in accordance with the times, places, and capacity of each (Examen 4.15 [70]).

Again there is the explicitly apostolic focus and, in addition, the indication that only those priests who have 'been tested and found edifying' will be sent on this experiment. Presumably this testing refers to the previous experiences. The priest-novice, if considered ready, is here inducted into the basic work of the Society, the ministry of word and sacrament.

Summary

As we said at the beginning of our reflections on the General Examen, its purpose is that the candidate may get to know the Society, and the Society get to know him. This twofold aim continues throughout the novitiate and the experiments play a central role in the process. The second element, that of the Society's getting to know the novice, is underlined in the ways that the General Examen proposes for investigating how the novice has conducted himself during the experiments. He who gives the Exercises must tell the superior what he thinks of the exercitant 'in regard to the end which the Society seeks' (Examen 4.18 [73]). From each of the other experiments the novice must be able to supply a testimony, not only that he has gone through the experience, but that he did so 'without a complaint from anyone', 'without offending anyone', but giving edification to all (Examen 4.18–22 [73–77]). In this way the wider Church plays its part in the Society's discernment concerning the novice's suitability for its ministerial life. All this meticulous concern shows the aim throughout the experiments of simultaneously testing and developing the apostolic capabilities of the novice.

---

[42] Ignatius to the Fathers of the Council of Trent, early 1546, Ignatius, *Letters*, 128–131.

What we have seen, therefore, is a series of experiments or experiences, not discrete but interrelated and forming a cohesive process. This process moves the novice from a search for devotion, the ability to find God in all things (the aim of the Spiritual Exercises in the novitiate), through experiences which call for humility, abnegation and poverty (the second, third and fourth experiences), to an explicit engagement in the ministerial life of the Society (the fifth and sixth experiences). It is an educative process whose principles mirror Christ's formation of his disciples in the Gospels, and also continue, *mutatis mutandis*, the pedagogy of the Spiritual Exercises themselves. Buckley draws together the strands of this whole dynamic:

> What are the six experiments attempting to test? First, whether someone can so be grasped by Christ that he can find God in all things—a charism essential to the Society, Nadal maintained; then, whether he has fundamentally achieved an independence from an atmospheric worldliness, whether he has broken definitively with what John's gospel calls the world; third, whether he can enter into a trusting poverty, a reliance upon a peculiar and pervasive providence which extends to the basic details of his life; fourth, whether he can conform and live in such a spirit within the ordinary, humdrum life of a Jesuit; and finally, whether he can do the ministerial service of the Society, can be of genuine assistance to others in catechetics, the sacraments, and the ministry of the word of God.[43]

Tertianship: Similarities and Differences

These experiences or experiments will be repeated during the third probation, usually known as the tertianship.[44] The General Examen reads:

---

[43] Buckley, 'Freedom, Election, and Self-Transcendence', 85–86. For Nadal's teaching on the experiments, and a discussion of early Jesuit practice, see Philip Endean, 'Origins of Apostolic Formation: Jerome Nadal and Novitiate Experiments', *The Way Supplement*, 39 (Summer 1980), 57–82. For the role they play today, see Paul Nicholson, 'Exercises, Experiments and Experiences: Tools for Ignatian Formation', *The Way*, 47/4 (October 2008), 77–92.

[44] See Anthony Ruhan, 'The Origins of the Jesuit Tertianship', in *Jesuit Spirit in a Time of Change*, edited by Raymond A. Schroth (Westminster, Md: Newman, 1967), 99–117.

> In the case of the scholastics, when their studies have been finished, in addition to the time of probation required to become an approved scholastic, before one of them makes profession or is admitted as a formed coadjutor, a further third year must be spent in passing through various probations, especially those tests mentioned above [Examen 4.9(64)] if he did not make them previously, and through some of them even if he did make them, for the greater glory of God (Examen 4.16[71]).

Further on, in part V, there is the well-known reference to the *schola affectus*, the school of the heart:

> For this purpose, it will be helpful for those who had been sent to studies, upon finishing the work and effort of intellectual formation, to apply themselves during the period of final probation to the school of the heart, exercising themselves in spiritual and corporal pursuits which can engender in them greater humility, abnegation of all sensual love and will and judgement of their own, and also greater knowledge and love of God our Lord; so that when they themselves have made progress they can better help others to progress for the glory of God our Lord (V.2.1[516]).

It will be clear from this passage that the Ignatian idea of repetition is again at work. The tertian will repeat the novitiate experiments but (as in the Exercises) with the goal of deepening these experiences at the level of affectivity or heart. The effects sought are no different in the tertianship than in the novitiate, so the only justification for this repetition is to allow these effects, these graces, to permeate at an ever deeper level the total personality of the Jesuit.

Of course the tertian is at a very different stage of his journey from the novice.[45] He is much more experienced in the ways of the spirit, and indeed in the ways of the world. Perhaps, therefore, the difference in the making of the experiments in the novitiate and in the tertianship reflects the difference between the Kingdom exercise and the Third Week. A younger man, moved by the call

---

[45] On some of the issues that arise in tertianship programmes today, see Frank J. Houdek, 'The Road Too Often Travelled: Formation: Developing the Apostolic Body of the Society', *Studies in the Spirituality of Jesuits*, 23/1 (1991).

of the King, goes out to conquer the whole world. He dreams, for instance, of being another Francis Xavier. The world seems waiting to be converted. That can be the mindset, the imaginative world, of the novice, eager to follow Christ in bringing the Good News to all peoples. The tertian, however, has a longer and more profound experience both of his own weakness and of the brokenness of even good-hearted people, the deafness, sloth and unwillingness of the world to hear the Good News. He is therefore more likely to experience his own vulnerability and helplessness during the experiments, as well as being more sensitive to the vulnerability and helplessness of others. He may well find himself called simply to be with others in their suffering, just as in the Spiritual Exercises the Third Week is an invitation to be with Jesus in his—nothing more, nothing less.[46]

---

[46] For a modern presentation of the purposes and way of making tertianship, see *Complementary Norms*, nn. 125–126, in *The Constitutions of the Society of Jesus and Their Complementary Norms*.

3.

AN APOSTOLIC LIFESTYLE UNDER VOWS

ANDRÉ DE JAER HAS ARGUED that the vows are to the *Constitutions* what the election is to the Exercises. He continues,

> The vows effect a fundamental transition. For the companion, his final vows are his assimilation into Jesus as he freely hands over his very life out of love, making a eucharist of it.[1] The Jesuit thus becomes one with Christ, who lives his paschal mystery, who was handed over freely out of love.[2]

Religious vows are never lived in a vacuum or in a purely spiritual state. They are always incarnated in particular persons within a particular historical and social context. So while a hermit, an anchoress, a monk, a cloistered nun, a friar, a canon regular, an apostolic sister or a Jesuit may make the same religious vows, the experience and expression of these vows will be different in each case. This is acknowledged in the commonly used formula by which vows are made 'according to the constitutions' of each institute. In the Society, therefore, the vows commit a person to live a life of consecrated chastity, obedience and poverty as a member of a body founded 'to help souls', that is, a body whose end is mission. The opening sentence of part VI points to this context when it says:

> In order that those already admitted to profession or as formed coadjutors may be able to employ themselves more fruitfully

---

[1] This act of making a eucharist of one's life is symbolized by the Jesuit practice of taking vows immediately before communion in the Mass, and facing the host upheld by the celebrant. See Peter-Hans Kolvenbach, 'On the 450th Anniversary of the Vows of Montmartre', *Acta Romana Societatis Iesu*, 19/1 (1988), 80–83; Noelle Hausmann, 'Pour la profession super hostiam: Une étude de la profession religieuse', *Nouvelle Revue Théologique*, 110 (1988), 729–742.

[2] André de Jaer, *Together for Mission: A Spiritual Commentary on the Constitutions of the Society of Jesus*, translated by Francis C. Brennan (St Louis: Institute of Jesuit Sources, 2001), 97. It is also possible to see the election of the Exercises as corresponding to the missioning (with its accompanying discernment and decision making) in part VII.

> according to our Institute in the service of God and the aid
> of their neighbours, they need to observe certain things in
> regard to themselves (*Constitutions* VI. 1. 1 [547]).

Hence the vows are in a sense instrumental. They are made
to enable a Jesuit to live out 'more fruitfully' his calling to
mission. This does not deny that each of the vows forms part of a
covenant between God and the individual and so has a uniquely
personal character. But the covenant into which God enters
with a Jesuit (and with the body of the Society) has mission
at its core. It is not possible to separate a Jesuit's religious vows
from his commitment to mission, any more than it is possible
to separate a Jesuit's prayer from that same commitment (see
below).

While the lifestyle of the professed is expressly dealt with in
part VI we cannot rely exclusively on what is said there in order
to understand Ignatius' teaching on the vows. This is because of
the developmental nature of the *Constitutions* which allows
Ignatius to treat the vows in ways that are appropriate to the
different stages of incorporation. Indeed, the whole sequence of
parts III to VI in particular needs to be kept in view as contributing
to a fuller explanation of the vows. The opening paragraph of
part III on the novitiate says:

> ... due consideration and provident care must be employed
> toward preserving in their vocation those who are being
> retained and tested in the houses or colleges, and toward
> enabling them to make progress both in spirit and in virtues
> along the path of the divine service (III. 1. 1 [243]).

This reference to virtues must include those that are required
in being faithful to the vows. Hence, in part III, chastity is treated
in III. 1. 4 [250], poverty in III. 1. 7–H [254–259] and III. 1. 25 [287],
and obedience in III. 1. 23–24 [284–286]. The teaching here is not
superseded by that in part VI but built on, developed, deepened
and applied in a new context. Part III is dealing with novices
whereas part VI presupposes persons who have been living the
vows over many years and have reached a further level of human
and spiritual maturity. They are also persons whose external
lifestyle is less structured than that of novices or scholastics in
studies.

Chastity

The only assertion that Ignatius makes concerning chastity begins with the words, 'What pertains to the vow of chastity requires no interpretation' (*Constitutions* VI. 1. 1 [547]). This statement generally provokes laughter and astonishment, as if it shows that Ignatius was naïve, prudish or simply ignorant. Linking this with his reference to angels in the second part of the sentence ('since it is evident how perfectly it should be preserved, by endeavouring to imitate therein the purity of the angels in cleanness of body and mind'), some accuse him of a disembodied idealism. Such an accusation is ludicrous. A few facts are worth examining briefly in order to situate chastity more adequately within Ignatius' broad vision of life.

The sentence in question appears for the first time in the final version of the *Constitutions* text (1556). It is even possible that Ignatius had no intention of discussing chastity at all, since neither text *a* nor text A of 1550 makes any mention of the subject. De Jaer comments, 'Very likely he inserted these few lines at the suggestion of the canonists, so that all three vows might be treated in part VI which deals with religious life'.[3] So why might he have thought of omitting this topic completely?

There is something foundational about chastity in Ignatius' own spiritual development. According to Laínez, Ignatius began his new life after his conversion with a vow of chastity shortly after leaving his ancestral home at Loyola.[4] Hence this vow predates his vigil at Montserrat and his eleven months of 'novitiate' at Manresa. From this time onward his total commitment to chastity was unquestioned. It remained so even when apostolic desires modified his motivation and gave a new focus to his spirituality and his life choices.[5]

---

[3] De Jaer, *Together for Mission*, 105–106. Of course the whole of the *Constitutions* (including the General Examen) deals with religious life, not just part VI. But it is clear what de Jaer means.

[4] See MHSJ FN 1, 74–77. The site of the vow was the Basque Marian shrine of Aránzazu, the first stop on Ignatius' journey to Montserrat. He had probably decided on the vow while convalescing in Loyola but, given his devotion to Our Lady, delayed pronouncing it until he could do so at Aránzazu. Laínez points to an element of fear or defensiveness in Ignatius at this point, claiming that he took the vow 'because he had more fear of being conquered in the area of chastity than in other things'.

[5] Laínez writes: 'He possesses chastity to a lofty degree, for he is very much in command of his own nature in purity of spirit; as though he feels nothing from the lower appetite',

Ignatius and his companions at the University of Paris (most probably) pronounced a vow of chastity at Montmartre in 1534. At this point the vow would have been associated in a general way with mission. They certainly made such a vow as they approached ordination at Venice in 1537. By then chastity was linked specifically with diaconate and priesthood, but not yet with membership of a religious order. This last link became operative when the companions pronounced their (first and) final *religious* vows in 1541.

It is curious, but not insignificant, that in the first *Formula of the Institute* (1540), chastity is the only vow mentioned in the opening paragraph.

> Whoever wishes to serve as a soldier of God beneath the banner of the cross in our Society, which we desire to be designated by the name of Jesus, and to serve the Lord alone and his vicar on earth, should keep in mind that once he has made a solemn vow of perpetual chastity he is a member of a community founded chiefly for this purpose .... (n. 1)

Again it may well have been the canonists who insisted on the addition of poverty and obedience to the corresponding paragraph in the *Formula* of 1550.

The main reason why the vow of chastity does not require interpretation is this. While poverty and obedience are unmistakably different in the Society from other religious orders, chastity is essentially the same. As we have remarked earlier, in the *Formula* and the *Constitutions* Ignatius devotes more space to what is different or novel in 'our way of proceeding' than to what is common to all religious. It is such innovative matters that need interpretation. Much of the rest can be taken as known.[6]

MHSJ FN 1, 140–141. The qualification 'as though' is important. Laínez is not saying that Ignatius felt no sexual movements but that he did not give in to them. See *Autobiography*, n. 10, quoted below, where Ignatius himself makes a similar claim reaching back to Loyola.

[6] Ignatius' thinking on how to treat chastity in the *Constitutions*, while understandable, is not satisfactory from a contemporary viewpoint. Though he can be absolved of ignorance or naïveté, he shares a reticence on the topic with writers of earlier religious legislation. For example, the rules of the Benedictines, Franciscans and Dominicans also mention chastity only briefly. For a contemporary presentation of Jesuit thinking, see decree 8 of

To return to the second part of Ignatius' sentence on chastity: '... it is evident how perfectly it should be preserved, by endeavouring to imitate therein the purity of the angels in cleanness of body and mind'.[7] One notes the careful use of words. Through their vow of *chastity* Jesuits are to endeavour to imitate the *purity* of the angels. Chastity and purity are not synonymous. It is only humans who can practise chastity. To have spoken of the chastity of the angels would have been a nonsense. But purity is a virtue or an attribute that both sexual and non-sexual beings can share. Purity denotes single-mindedness, a clarity of vision and simplicity of intention, an undividedness of heart and will. Such purity is experienced and expressed by the angels according to their entirely spiritual nature, and by human persons according to their spiritual-corporeal nature.[8] For those who are given this gift, the commitment of religious chastity is a powerful way of expressing and living this purity. In other words, human sexuality itself can become the vehicle for (quite literally) giving a body to the spirit of single-mindedness that is purity.

But even more is hidden behind Ignatius' text. The theology of the angels was much more prominent and highly developed through the Middle Ages and into the sixteenth century than it is today. While convalescing at Loyola, Ignatius would have read in Ludolph of Saxony's *Life of Christ:*

> Because human beings are to be associated with the blessed spirits, everyone in the Church, and especially in religion, should minister to others faithfully, humbly, and devoutly. Those who for God's sake come with brotherly love to the aid of the sick and of pilgrims, or of the poor and one another are in the first rank and are like the angels. Those who seek to be more familiar with God in prayer and strive to help their neighbour through teaching, counselling,

the 34th Jesuit General Congregation, 'Chastity in the Society of Jesus', *Jesuit Life and Mission Today*, 576–588.

[7] In what follows I draw on the monograph by Joseph F. Conwell, 'Living and Dying in the Society of Jesus or Endeavouring to Imitate Angelic Purity', *Studies in the Spirituality of Jesuits*, 12/3 (1980).

[8] Compare the phrase 'my whole self as composed of soul and body' in Exx 47.

and other help are in the second rank and are like the archangels.[9]

The author goes on to draw further parallels between all the choirs of angels on the one hand and human beings on the other, in their relationship with God and their role in God's plan for his creation. In the understanding of the medieval tradition the angelic life is composed of contemplation and ministry. The purity of the angels, therefore, is a stance of openness towards God (contemplation), and openness to God's will (ministry). It combines a loving readiness or availability to be constantly before God's throne, in God's presence, and also to go anywhere and do anything at God's request. And yet (and here I imagine is what was most congenial to Ignatius in this theology), even in ministry, even when sent abroad, the angels never depart from God's presence. Angels are the perfect 'contemplatives in action'.

For one final insight into Ignatius' understanding of chastity we return to the beginnings of his conversion experience at Loyola as recorded in the *Autobiography*.

> His greatest desire, after regaining his health, was to go to Jerusalem, as previously stated, and to observe the fasts and to practise the discipline as any generous soul on fire with God is accustomed to do. With these holy desires of his, the thoughts of his former life were soon forgotten and this was confirmed by a vision in this manner. One night, as he lay sleepless, he clearly saw the likeness of our Lady with the holy Child Jesus, and because of this vision he enjoyed an excess of consolation for a remarkably long time. He felt so great a loathsomeness for all his past life, especially for the deeds of the flesh, that it seemed to him that all the images that had been previously imprinted on his mind were now erased. Thus from that hour until August 1553 when this is being written, he never again consented, not even in the least matter, to the motions of the flesh. (nn. 9–10)

This experience brought Ignatius healing and freedom in the area of sexuality. However, what is particularly notable is that this

---

[9] Ludolph of Saxony, *Life of Christ*, volume 2, chapter 6. Cited in Conwell, 'Living and Dying', 8.

healing and freedom is explicitly linked with Ignatius' desire and determination to go on pilgrimage to Jerusalem. It is as if chastity becomes possible, falls into place and is integrated into his personality, precisely when the call to pilgrimage gives a focus to his life and sets its parameters. Pilgrimage to Jerusalem implies a separation, a voluntary exile from family, home and country, and as such is a sign of the *eschaton,* that final age when there will be neither marrying nor giving in marriage.

Temporary celibate chastity is the most appropriate mode of sexuality for a temporary pilgrimage. Lifelong celibate chastity is the most appropriate mode of sexuality for a lifelong pilgrimage. Like the angel sent by God, the pilgrim (who also experiences himself or herself as sent) is totally absorbed in the pilgrimage itself and its goal. So when Ignatius comes to write the *Constitutions* he carries with him this (by now inherent) sense of his life as a pilgrimage, but also of the evangelical life of the Society as a pilgrimage. He does not feel any need to explain how chastity is appropriate for this journey. He himself had become aware of its value from the earliest days of his conversion. He presumes that Jesuits have had a similar experience.[10]

Obedience

Ignatius uses the statement on chastity as an introduction to what he wants to say about obedience. He writes, 'Therefore, with this [teaching on chastity] presupposed, we shall now treat of holy obedience' (VI.1.1[547]). This was the chronology through which he and the First Companions came to obedience. They were first consecrated through chastity, later they discerned that they were also called to consecrate themselves through obedience.[11] One might speculate as to whether in the mind of the later Ignatius chastity–obedience constituted a single reality.[12]

---

[10] 'It is easy to see, therefore, why Ignatius, who is not a harsh man, is very hard on those who fail in chastity. Unchastity is a distraction from the pilgrimage and the mission. The unchaste have been derailed; they have lost their orientation; they are going nowhere as far as the pilgrimage or mission is concerned.' (Conwell, 'Living and Dying', 14)

[11] Their attraction to poverty probably coincided with that to chastity.

[12] See Conwell, 'Living and Dying', 17.

If one accepts the interpretation of chastity that I have offered, obedience and chastity are concerned with many of the same values: being on pilgrimage, being sent, being contemplative, centring one's whole life on God. From the total availability of the angels (what we have called their purity)—their readiness to go anywhere at the least sign of God's will—we already have some basic idea of the core of Jesuit obedience. All that is said of the purity of the angels must be incarnated, enfleshed, not only through the living of one's sexuality (relationships), but through obedience, poverty, work and even (as in part VI, chapter 4) through illness and death. From the perspective of formation this process of enfleshment is marked, as we would expect, by movement. Ignatius sees the need for a certain rigidity when the Jesuit is young and inexperienced, moving towards greater suppleness when he is mature and onwards to a free abandonment of self at the moment of death.

While Jesuit obedience is distinctive, Ignatius learnt much from a broader theology of obedience—Christian and religious. He realised that it is a virtue with many dimensions. Four of these are especially noteworthy and can be discovered throughout the pages of the *Constitutions*: the ascetical, mystical, unitive and apostolic dimensions.[13] In brief:

- The *ascetical* dimension refers to the need for human effort, the overcoming of difficulties and resistances, the exercising of the virtue of obedience and being exercised in it, and finally the process of its becoming a habit.

- The *mystical* dimension is the experience of God in the practice of obedience. It embraces the grace to recognise the authority of Christ in the authority of the superior and the person of Christ in the person of the superior. It also includes the experience of one's obedience as a participation in the obedience of Jesus to his Father.

- The *unitive* dimension underlines the effectiveness of obedience as a unifying element in the body of the Society.

[13] See Brian O'Leary, 'Christian and Religious Obedience', in *Paths of Renewal for Religious*, edited by David L. Fleming (St Louis: Review for Religious, 1986), 195–201.

More than any other means it creates good order and deep bonding. It assures the corporate nature of Jesuit mission.

- The *apostolic* dimension sees obedience as uniting the Jesuit with the saving will of God for God's people. It understands that mission is the *raison d'être* of the Society and it brings about the individual Jesuit's insertion into that mission.

While these four dimensions are always present, the *Constitutions* emphasize each of them to a greater or lesser extent, and with different nuances, according to the developmental stage of the Jesuit in his incorporation into the Society. The ascetical and mystical dimensions are accented more in the General Examen and part III (in the context of initial formation) and in part VI (in the context of the life of the professed). The apostolic dimension comes to the fore in the treatment of missioning in part VII, and the unitive element naturally predominates in part VIII, on union of minds and hearts.

It follows, therefore, that although part VI contains a profound presentation of obedience as understood by Ignatius, it is still a partial account. It focuses on the attitudes, intentionality and feelings of the individual professed Jesuit. But however rich this exposition, it needs to be complemented by the more corporate insights both of union (part VIII) and of mission (part VII) for it to be fully Ignatian.

Ignatius understood obedience as central to Jesuit identity, and somehow distinctive of it. He wrote a series of letters on the subject in response to difficulties that were arising in Spain and Portugal. The last of these became known as 'The Letter on Obedience' and for some centuries assumed an importance greater than the more rounded teaching on the subject in the *Constitutions*. It contains the well-known paragraph:

> We may let other religious orders outdo us in fasting, night-watches, and other austerities which each one, following its own institute, holily observes. But in the purity and perfection of obedience, with genuine resignation of our wills and abnegation of our judgment, I am very desirous, dear brothers, that those who serve God in this Society should distinguish themselves, and that its true sons may be recognised by this—never looking to the person whom they

obey, but in that person, to Christ our Lord, for whose sake
they obey.[14]

This letter is polemical in intent, rhetorical in style and
ascetical in its emphases.[15] Few would claim today that its account
of obedience is what is distinctive of the Society. We need to
look to the broader and more elaborate conception of obedience
that is rooted in the Spiritual Exercises and elaborated in the
different parts of the *Constitutions*. That obedience, with *discreta
caritas* at its core and mission as its main object, is certainly
distinctive of the Jesuit way of proceeding.

Poverty

The second chapter of part VI deals with poverty. We recall the
early enthusiasm of Ignatius, as recorded in the *Autobiography*,
for the extreme asceticism of the Desert Fathers as well as for
the mendicant spirit of Francis and Dominic. But during his
protracted stay at Manresa he experienced a shift from the
attraction of solitary mendicancy to that of apostolic mendicancy.
He began to live this more outgoing expression of an evangelical
life during his pilgrimage to Jerusalem, and even (eventually more
corporately) during his years of study. Perhaps the simplest
expression of this ideal occurs in a letter he wrote from Venice
in 1536 to his benefactor Jaime Cassador. The latter had been
urging him to return and preach in Barcelona. Ignatius expresses
his desire to do so provided God does not call him elsewhere.
He writes, 'I am not sure which [location] it will be; but certainly
my state will be that of preaching in poverty, with none of the
abundance or encumbrances I now have during my studies'.[16]

As he gathered companions, especially those he met at the
University of Paris, he shared with them his enthusiasm for

---

[14] Ignatius to the Members of the Society in Portugal, 26 March 1553, Ignatius, *Letters*,
412–421, at 413.
[15] A helpful presentation and critique of the series of letters on obedience is that by
John C. Futrell, *Making an Apostolic Community of Love: The Role of the Superior
according to St Ignatius of Loyola* (St Louis: Institute of Jesuit Sources, 1970), 195–213.
[16] Jaime Cassador was archdeacon and later archbishop of Barcelona. He had been one of
the most generous benefactors of Ignatius during his studies in Paris. Ignatius obviously
felt under obligation to him. See Ignatius, *Letters*, 15–16.

living gospel poverty. After their ordination the companions modelled this poor apostolic life (the life of the apostles) in the months they spent in Venice and the towns of northern Italy. After the Deliberation of 1539, when Ignatius came to compose the document that eventually became the *Formula of the Institute*, he appealed to his own and the companions' prior experience when he introduced the topic of poverty. This explicit reference to experience rather than to the *magisterium* or tradition is significant. The companions already knew existentially the value of living in poverty. The *Formula* (1550) reads:

> From experience we have learned that a life removed as far as possible from all infection of avarice and as like as possible to evangelical poverty is more gratifying, more undefiled, and more suitable for the edification of our neighbours. We likewise know that our Lord Jesus Christ will supply to his servants who are seeking only the kingdom of God what is necessary for food and clothing. Therefore our members, one and all, should vow perpetual poverty .... (n.7)

In the *Constitutions* poverty is described with two contrasting metaphors: as a mother, and (using a cluster of images) as a strong wall, a defence, a rampart and a bulwark. The first image is used in part III with the novices: 'All should love poverty as a mother, and according to the measure of holy discretion all should, when occasions arise, feel some of its effects' (III.1.25[287]). Addressing the professed in part VI, Ignatius writes:

> Poverty, as the strong wall of the religious institute, should be loved and preserved in its integrity as far as this is possible with God's grace. The enemy of the human race generally tries to weaken this defence and rampart which God our Lord inspired religious institutes to raise against him and the other adversaries of their perfection. (VI.2.1[553])

The same imagery and teaching reappear in part X:

> Since poverty is like a bulwark of religious institutes which preserves them in their existence and good order and defends them from many enemies, and since the devil uses corresponding effort to destroy this bulwark in one way or another, it will be highly important for the preservation and growth of this whole body that every appearance of avarice should be banished afar ... (X.5[816]).

Ignatius is aware that the spiritual well-being of religious institutes has always been dependent on, and to some extent proportionate to, their practice of poverty. In the monastic tradition, when an abbey became too affluent and wealthy religious observance went into decline. There followed, with something approaching inevitability, one of two consequences: either the disintegration of the monastery or a reform that reinstated authentic poverty (by returning to the group's original tradition). Hence the need for constant vigilance expressed here in the martial imagery with which we are familiar from the Spiritual Exercises. Poverty is a strong defensive wall to be used against 'the enemy of the human race'. But it is to be noted that Ignatius twice encourages the members of his institute to love poverty. This is less surprising when he is using the metaphor of poverty as a mother, but he continues to exhort to a love of poverty even when the metaphor is impersonal (the wall, etc.). The way of poverty is not just an ascetical discipline or a practice that has a pragmatic usefulness, but is an expression of our relationship with Christ. It thrives so long as it is loved; when it ceases to be loved it may be tolerated for a while, but eventually it will simply fade away.

In the above passages we already see some of the motivations for poverty as intrinsic to Jesuit life. Many others appear throughout the *Constitutions*.

- Some are theological and christological, for example 'in conformity with the counsels of Christ our Lord' (III.1.7 [254]), 'for the love of God our Lord' (Examen 4.12[67]), 'to serve God totally' (Examen 4.1[53]), 'to the glory of God our Lord' (III.1.9[258]), 'place his reliance entirely in his Creator and Lord' (Examen 4.12[67], VI.2.2[555]), 'our reward should be only Christ our Lord' (IV.15.4[478]).

- Others are ascetical.

- Still more are related to mission, for example, edification of the neighbour (not only witness but, in today's language, credibility) (III.1.9[258], VI.2.7[565], VI.3.16[580]), or apostolic freedom (stemming from a commitment to gratuity of ministries) (VI.2.7[565]).

What is most striking is the absence of the key motivation for poverty that we find in the Spiritual Exercises, that is, love of the poor Christ and desire to be with him in his poverty. We recall the colloquies of the Kingdom (Exx 98) and the Two Standards (Exx 147), and the description of the Third Way of Being Humble (Exx 167). This last is a reality when,

> ... in order to imitate Christ our Lord better and to be more like him here and now, I desire and choose poverty with Christ poor rather than wealth; contempt with Christ laden with it rather than honours. Even further, I desire to be regarded as a useless fool for Christ, who before me was regarded as such, rather than as a wise and prudent person in this world.

Here Ignatius vividly spells out the consequences of poverty in terms of how the world views the poor, who are treated as of no importance, as nonentities, as fools. Such was the way chosen by Christ in his lifetime. In the *Constitutions*, however, this motivation for poverty (as desire to be with the poor and suffering Christ) is not mentioned but is certainly presumed. The *Constitutions*, as we have seen, are addressed to persons who have already received the graces of the Exercises.[17]

There is, however, one passage in the *Constitutions* that explores this core dimension of poverty, even while not using the word itself. This is the passage in chapter 4 of the General Examen that we described previously as an exposition of the Third Way of Being Humble.

> Just as the men of the world who follow the world love and seek with such great diligence honours, fame, and esteem for a great name on earth, as the world teaches them, so those who proceed spiritually and truly follow Christ our Lord love and intensely desire everything opposite. That is to say, they desire to clothe themselves with the same garb and uniform of their Lord because of the love and reverence owed to him,

---

[17] Approaching this issue in another way Michael Ivens writes, 'First, the meaning of actual poverty is, at once and inseparably, both personal and apostolic. In its personal aspect, poverty is founded in the desires which constitute the grace of the Second Week of the Exercises; in its apostolic aspect it forms an integral part of the Jesuit's service of the kingdom .... The concept of poverty developed in the *Constitutions* is that of the Exercises, and in the Exercises the desire to be poor in order to "go against" the dynamisms of self-interest and to be personally Christlike is inextricably bound up with the desire to share the work of Christ in the world.' ('Poverty in the *Constitutions* and Other Ignatian Sources', *The Way Supplement,* 61 [Spring 1988], 76–88, at 77)

to such an extent that where there would be no offence to
his Divine Majesty and no imputation of sin to the neighbour,
they desire to suffer injuries, false accusations, and affronts,
and to be held and esteemed as fools (but without their giving
any occasion for this), because of their desire to resemble
and imitate in some manner our Creator and Lord Jesus
Christ, by putting on his garb and uniform, since it was
for our spiritual profit that he clothed himself as he did.
(Examen 4.44[101])

Turning finally to the practical living out of such desires,
Ignatius in part VI gives us the conclusions to his own long
discernment on the poverty of the Society (recorded in his *Spiritual
Diary*). There are to be two types of poverty among Jesuits,
depending on where they live. In the houses of the professed[18]
the poverty is that of strict mendicancy, while in the colleges
the style of poverty is an adaptation of the monastic model. In
simple terms the difference is between having no fixed revenues
and being allowed fixed revenues. Those living in the houses of
the professed must live on alms, but those living in colleges are
allowed to benefit from fixed revenues because of the need to
support those in formation.[19]

Even though poverty can never be an absolute value in an
institute whose end is mission, nevertheless Ignatius makes it
clear that he wants actual poverty to be experienced in so far as
this is possible. He is well aware of how easy it is to be deceived in
this area, as the exercise on Two Standards illustrates. Aiming
at spiritual poverty while bypassing actual poverty will end by
our missing both. In a well-known letter in praise of poverty,
commissioned by Ignatius though written by Polanco, we read:

> I will only add this: Lovers of poverty should also love her
> retinue as far as they can—poor food, poor clothing, poor
> sleeping accommodations, and being looked down upon.

---

[18] These are residences where the professed Jesuits are given totally to ministry. They
are living the life of the apostles.
[19] The living out of poverty is probably more variable than that of any other aspect of
religious life. Since professed houses soon died out almost completely in the Society, it
could be said that Ignatius' own legislation was effective over a short period only. Different
economic systems call for changing legislation and practice of poverty, and the Society
has been forced constantly to update its thinking on the matter.

> Otherwise, someone who loved poverty but was unwilling to experience any deprivation or effect of it would be a pretty dainty poor person. He would certainly give evidence that he loved the name rather than the reality of poverty—or loved it with words more than with the heart.[20]

In this scathing section of the letter Ignatius/Polanco is only echoing the warnings of the earlier Christian tradition. A similarly caustic passage (one of many) appears in a letter from Bernard of Clairvaux to William, abbot of the wealthy Benedictine abbey of Cluny. But Bernard adds a series of examples, full of psychological insight, into how religious can rationalise their breaches of poverty. In Ignatian terms he illustrates how the evil spirit can deceive us by posing as an angel of light.

> Abstemiousness is accounted miserliness, sobriety strictness, silence gloom. On the other hand, laxity is labelled discretion, extravagance generosity, talkativeness sociability, and laughter joy. Fine clothes and costly caparisons are regarded as mere respectability, and being fussy about bedding is hygiene. When we lavish these things on one another, we call it love. Such love undermines true love. Such discretion disgraces real discretion. This sort of kindness is full of cruelty, for it so looks after the body that the soul is strangled.[21]

Prayer in the *Constitutions*

A puzzling aspect of the *Constitutions* is the paucity of teaching on prayer. It is quite impossible to answer the question 'What is Jesuit prayer?' from examining the *Constitutions* on their own. Even by spreading our net more widely than the *Constitutions* (looking at the *Autobiography*, the *Spiritual Exercises*, the *Spiritual Diary* and the letters), this question about the nature of Jesuit prayer leads to conclusions that are by no means clear or totally coherent. We are aware of the early controversies in the Society between the 'ascetics' and the 'mystics'.[22] These controversies

---

[20] Ignatius to the members of the Society in Padua, 7 August 1547, Ignatius, *Letters*, 203–207, here 206–207.

[21] Bernard of Clairvaux, 'An Apologia to Abbot William', in *Treatises I* (Shannon: Irish UP, 1970), 52–53.

[22] See Robert E. McNally, 'St Ignatius: Prayer and the Early Society of Jesus', *Woodstock Letters*, 94 (1965), 109–134; Paul Begheyn, 'The Controversies on Prayer after the Death

rumble on although not often acknowledged openly today. From another perspective it might be argued that Jesuit prayer is very much psychologically and culturally conditioned. Is it as much an expression of an individual's personality and ethnic/cultural make-up as of some distinctive Jesuit tradition?

What is not in doubt is that Jesuit prayer cannot be understood outside a context of mission. But the link between prayer and mission is complex.[23] These difficult issues challenge us to integrate the evidence of *all* the Ignatian sources and the lived experience of the Society. However, that broader canvas is beyond the scope of our present explorations, which will be concentrating mostly on the *Constitutions*.

The first point that strikes one is the *oblique* way in which Ignatius deals with prayer in this document. He does not offer precise teaching or guidance on how to pray, but rather on how to create the preconditions and interior dispositions in which prayer may take place. So he will encourage mortification, purity of intention, the cultivation of desires, the practice of virtue, and so on, and then presume that a person living this kind of life will know intuitively how to relate with God at times of formal prayer. Ignatius calls people to integrity and to interiority. He believes that such integrity and interiority will both lead to prayer and in turn be nourished by it. And, of course, he presumes that the Jesuit has made the Spiritual Exercises.

---

of Ignatius and their Effect on the Concept of Jesuit Mission', in *CIS*, 72, *History and Spirituality of the Society of Jesus* (1993), 78–93; Joseph Veale, 'Ignatian Prayer or Jesuit Spirituality', in *Manifold Gifts*, 150–160; Philip Endean, 'The Original Line of Our Father Ignatius: Mercurian and the Spirituality of the Exercises' and 'This Strange Style of Prayer: Mercurian, Cordeses, and Alvarez', in *The Mercurian Project: Forming Jesuit Culture 1573–1580*, edited by Thomas M. McCoog (Rome: IHSI and St Louis: Institute of Jesuit Sources, 2004), 35–48, 351–397.

[23] Pierre Favre pondered on this issue in his *Memoriale*: 'Reflecting the same day on how to pray well and on different ways of doing good, I wondered how holy desires in prayer are, as it were, ways of disposing us to perform good works and, on the other hand, how good works lead us to good desires. I then noted, indeed clearly perceived, that, by seeking God in good works through the spirit, one will more readily find him afterwards in prayer than if one had sought him first in prayer so as to find him subsequently in good works, as is often done.' (n.126) This begins a long reflection that extends to n.129. (Pierre Favre, *Memoriale*, translated by Edmond C. Murphy, in *The Spiritual Writings of Pierre Favre: The Memoriale and Selected Letters and Instructions* [St Louis: Institute of Jesuit Sources, 1996], 141–144, here 141.)

Nadal, who was Ignatius' favoured interpreter of the *Constitutions*, wrote: 'Not so much is said in the *Constitutions* about prayer precisely because they take it for granted that the Exercises have already been made'.[24] And elsewhere: 'It is in the Exercises that Jesuits are shown and taught the path of prayer'.[25]

The second point that stands out, and is already familiar to us from other contexts, is that the developmental nature of the *Constitutions* leads Ignatius to treat prayer differently when dealing with novices, scholastics in studies, and the formed or professed members. We recall the text of the Preamble:

> ... inasmuch as this body is made up of its members, and what occurs first in the order of execution pertains to the individual members, in regard to their admission, progress, and distribution into the vineyard of Christ our Lord, it is from this consideration that we shall begin ... (Preamble 2[135]).

Here the generic word 'progress' has to include progress in prayer. But their progress in prayer will be linked with their overall growth in maturity as well as in all aspects of their life in the Society—leading up to and subsequent to their 'distribution into the vineyard of Christ our Lord'. We need to be aware of this principle of adaptability as Ignatius speaks of Jesuits at different stages of incorporation. Let us follow the sequence he offers us.

We turn first to those in their first probation, the *novices*.

> All should strive to keep their intention right, not only in regard to their state of life but also in all particular details in which they should aim always at serving and pleasing the Divine Goodness for its own sake and because of the incomparable love and benefits with which he has anticipated us, rather than for fear of punishments or hope of rewards, although they ought to draw help from these also. They should often be exhorted to seek God our Lord in all things, removing from themselves as far as possible love of all creatures in order to place it in the Creator of them, loving him in all creatures and all creatures in him, in conformity with his holy and divine will. (III. 1.26[288])

[24] MHSJ MN 5, 95.
[25] MHSJ MN 5, 484.

So, in summary form, the novices are exhorted to foster:

- a right intention in everything;

- a seeking of God in everything;

- a freeing of themselves from disordered attachments;

- all in order to love God totally;

- loving God in God's world and God's world in God.

When we come to the *scholastics in studies*, the approach is fundamentally the same, but adapted to their changed living and work situation:

> However, once they have satisfactorily completed them [the probations or experiments) and are devoting themselves to studies, while care must be taken that through fervour in study they do not grow cool in their love of true virtues and of religious life, still they will not at that time have much place for mortifications or for long prayers and meditations. For their devoting themselves to learning, which they acquire with a pure intention of serving God and which in a certain way requires the whole person, will be not less but rather more pleasing to God our Lord during this time of study. (IV.4.2[340])

And, in a later chapter:

> In order to make good progress in these subjects, the scholastics should strive first of all to keep their souls pure and their intention in studying right, by seeking in their studies nothing except the glory of God and the good of souls. Moreover, they should frequently beg in prayer for grace to make progress in learning for the sake of this end. (IV.6.1[360])

So, in summary form, the scholastics are asked to cultivate:

- a general purity of soul; a right intention of serving God through their studies; a total dedication to studies, which require the whole person;

- a conviction that God is more pleased by their rightly motivated studies than by long prayers;

- prayer for progress in their studies.

This last requirement is the only reference to a way of praying or a content for prayer, apart from some references in IV.4.3–B[342–343] to liturgical prayers, the Hours of Our Lady and the examination of conscience.

Finally we come to part VI and the prayer of the professed.

> Given the length of time and approbation of their life which are required before admission into the Society among the professed and also the formed coadjutors, it is presupposed that those so admitted will be men who are spiritual and sufficiently advanced that they will run in the path of Christ our Lord to the extent that their bodily strength and the exterior occupations undertaken through charity and obedience allow. Therefore, in what pertains to prayer, meditation, and study, and also in regard to the bodily practices of fasts, vigils, and other austerities or penances, *it does not seem proper to give them any other rule than that which discreet charity dictates to them*, provided that the confessor always be informed, and also, when a doubt about advisability arises, the superior. Only this will be said in general: *On the one hand, they should take care that the excessive use of these practices not weaken their bodily strength and take up so much time that they are rendered incapable of helping the neighbour spiritually according to our Institute; on the other hand, they should be vigilant that these practices not be relaxed to such an extent that the spirit grows cold and the human and lower passions grow warm.* (VI.3.1[582], my emphases)

This magisterial paragraph is more difficult to summarise. However, we might pick out some salient features:

- the long period of formation has brought the professed to the point of being 'spiritual', in other words, filled with the Spirit;

- this allows them to guide themselves in the matter of prayer through *discreta caritas*, discreet or discerning love;

- a confessor, spiritual director or superior aids such discernment;

- a criterion to be always kept in mind is the charism of the Institute, 'helping the neighbour spiritually';

- this criterion will allow one to reach a balance between excess and neglect in the matter of prayer (and penances).

We might notice how the familiar Ignatian theme of movement is taken up in the metaphor of 'running in the path of Christ our Lord'. In the matter of prayer the professed do not crawl, or walk or stumble along! They run with the grace and strength of a top-class long-distance athlete. A person with a well-conditioned body which has reached the peak of its fitness and potential now enjoys a freedom and exhilaration of movement unknown to those who have never exercised their bodies with regularity and intensity. Similarly the professed, who have been spiritually exercised over many years, are seen as enjoying an ease and a freedom of spiritual movement outside the experience of those still in formation. They do not need superiors or legislation to spur them on or help them to keep going. If anything they may need to be restrained and reminded of the true end and goal of the Society which is 'to help souls'.

Whether such restraint is needed in the Society (or elsewhere) today is dubious. The *Constitutions* here may presume too much and be reflective of the religious climate of the sixteenth century. We have seen how long hours of prayer were taken for granted as requirements for holiness and that the relatively modest amount of formal prayer in the Society's legislation was a scandal to some of its critics. Ignatius seems to fear that Jesuits, even when professed, may feel drawn to extended periods of prayer that would be inimical to their apostolic commitments. Such fear was not unfounded, as he already had to deal with the (admittedly extreme) cases of Oviedo and Onfroy. Polanco writes:

> It happened that the inclination of both Father Andrea de Oviedo and François Onfroy toward the internal practice of things spiritual was so powerful that Father Ignatius felt it absolutely necessary to apply moderation. Father Andrea himself wrote that over and above the time he spent in reciting the Divine Office, he devoted at least three more hours daily to prayer and, depending on the number of official duties that demanded his attention on a given day, he spent more than three additional hours in this practice …. Sometimes his inclination … reached such a stage that he no longer wished to have any dealings with his neighbour if he could help it,

except insofar as obedience or God's inspiration or at least right reason obliged him to engage in them; the rest of his time he desired to give to contemplation and prayer. Father François Onfroy, as the duke himself [Borgia] wrote to Rome, began at midnight and devoted seven continuous hours to prayer. The situation finally reached the point that, motivated by a great impulse of the spirit, they both aspired to retreat to a desert.[26]

We return now to the *Constitutions*.[27] Of the three developmental stages (those of novices, scholastics and professed) it is the way in which Ignatius deals with Jesuits in studies that best permits us to follow the kind of logic he brings to the topic of prayer. In fact, grasping what he is trying to engender in scholastics is the only way of understanding his apparently laissez faire legislation for the prayer of the professed.

However, as a starting-point we need to revisit the purpose of the Exercises in the novitiate.

> Likewise, care should be taken both that they learn what is proper and not let it be forgotten, and that they put what they have learned into practice, all of them devoting time to spiritual things and striving to acquire devotion to the extent that divine grace imparts it to them. Toward this purpose, it will be helpful to give all or some of the Spiritual Exercises to those who have not made them, as may be judged expedient for them in our Lord. (III.1.20[277])

In discussing the General Examen we already made some brief comments on the meaning of *devoción*, drawing attention to Ignatius' succinct definition in the *Autobiography*: '... his devotion, that is, his ease in finding God, was always increasing, now more than ever in his entire life. At whatever time or hour he wanted to find God, he found Him.' (n.99) This ease in finding God is what the novices are expected to acquire through various experiences (the Exercises, supplemented and confirmed by the

---

[26] *Year by Year with the Early Jesuits: Selections from the 'Chronicon' of Juan de Polanco*, translated and annotated by John Patrick Donnelly (St Louis: Institute of Jesuit Sources, 2004), 84–85. References to Ignatius' letters on this issue were given in chapter 2.
[27] In what follows I have again drawn on Buckley, 'Freedom, Election, and Self-Transcendence'.

other experiments) and the professed are presumed to have already acquired and to enjoy. This too is what Ignatius tries to help the scholastics to hold on to, in spite of difficulties that are specific to those who study.

One might well argue that the phrase 'ease in finding God' is just as obscure as the word 'devotion'. Although many people today throw such phrases around rather glibly (even more 'finding God in all things') it is questionable if they always know what they mean! It often happens that a person who claims to be finding God is really finding the Self. Or meeting an idol, a God made in his or her own image rather than the God of Abraham, Isaac and Jacob—the Father of the Lord Jesus Christ.[28]

Ignatius does not deal with such difficulties, which are more typical (at least in their articulation) of the psychologized world of the twentieth and twenty-first centuries than of his own time. But he is conscious of other obstacles to devotion, and is especially sensitive to those experienced by scholastics in studies. In some letters that have scholastics particularly in mind he spells out in greater detail what he stated briefly in the *Constitutions*. In a response to questions posed to him by the Portuguese scholastic Antonio Brandão, he writes:

> ... they can practice seeking the presence of our Lord in all things: in their dealings with other people, their walking, seeing, tasting, hearing, understanding, and all our activities. For his Divine Majesty truly is in everything by his presence, power, and essence. This kind of meditation—finding God our Lord in everything—is easier than lifting ourselves up and laboriously making ourselves present to more abstracted divine realities. Moreover, by making us properly disposed, this excellent exercise will bring great visitations of our Lord even in a short prayer.[29]

[28] Franz Meures ends a trenchant critique of the contemporary use of this slogan with the statement: 'From this perspective I consider it no accident that in the first four hundred years of Ignatian tradition the key expression "finding God in all things" is seldom to be found as a heading for Ignatian spirituality. This has happened only in the last thirty to forty years. This expression points out very well the goal of the spiritual way, but, precisely because it fits so well with our time, it can be poison for beginners.' ('The Spiritual Exercises as Biography', *The Way*, 47/1–2 [January and April 2008], 185–199, here 199.

[29] Ignatius to Antonio Brandão, 1 June 1551, Ignatius, *Letters*, 339–345 here 342. The heading of this letter shows that it was not meant solely for the Portuguese scholastics.

We are immediately reminded of the Contemplation to Attain Love, its second point—'I will consider how God dwells in creatures ... in the elements ... in the plants ... in the animals ... in human beings ... in myself' (Exx 235)—and its third point—'I will consider how God labours and works for me in all the creatures on the face of the earth ... in the heavens, elements, plants, fruits, cattle, and all the rest' (Exx 236). That important *et cetera* embraces the 'creatures' or 'things' that he mentions in the letter: both the objects of our looking, tasting, hearing, understanding and so forth, and those human experiences of walking, looking, tasting, hearing and understanding themselves. If I see a tree I am to find God in that tree (dwelling and labouring) as well as in my act of seeing (in which God also dwells and labours). It is not a matter of reasoning about God's presence and activity, but an intuitive acknowledgement that I am immersed in that reality, that mystery. Out of this experience comes the reverence that is Ignatius' habitual manner of reacting to people, things and God.[30]

This way of finding God in creation, *en todas las cosas*, and in our sensual, affective, imaginative and intellectual response to creation, is contrasted by Ignatius with the practice of 'lifting ourselves up and laboriously making ourselves present to more abstracted divine realities'. By this he seems to mean the meditation on or contemplation of God in Godself, or the truths of Christian faith that are less tangible and call for speculative thought. This can be a more difficult, even a more burdensome way to pray, especially for those who are already committed to full-time studies. The mind needs a rest and prayer is a good place to seek such a rest. This is not simply an easy option but rather an adaptation of the requirement of prayer to the needs of the scholastic.

It is significant that all the examples Ignatius uses are of secular realities, both in the Contemplation to Attain Love and in the letter to Brandão. But the term 'secular', as we might understand

It reads: 'Instructions given by our Father Ignatius, or at his direction, to those living outside Rome, and other significant matters that should not be forgotten'.
[30] *Acatamiento* (veneration, reverence, respect). See Charles E. O'Neill, '*Acatamiento*: Ignatian Reverence in History and in Contemporary Culture', *Studies in the Spirituality of Jesuits*, 8/1 (1976).

it today would not be a category in his own thought. For him all things (*todas las cosas*) are creatures, flow from God's hands and are in essential relationship with God. He does not ever think of creatures/things without an awareness of the God who dwells and labours in them, nor does he ever think of God without an awareness of the creatures/things in which God dwells and labours. To be constantly aware of this God, so close as well as so transcendent, is to 'pray at all times', to live in *le milieu divin*.

Apart from this general teaching on searching for and finding God in the ordinariness of life, Ignatius addresses the particular difficulties raised by study itself. In part IV of the *Constitutions* he insists on purity of intention:

> Next, they should have a firm resolution to be genuine and earnest students, persuading themselves that while they are in the colleges they cannot do anything more pleasing to God our Lord than to study with the intention mentioned above; likewise, that even if they never have occasion to employ the matter studied, the very toil of study, duly undertaken because of charity and obedience, is itself a very meritorious work in the sight of the Divine and Supreme Majesty (IV.6.2[361]).

This last comment would seem to indicate that, even in Ignatius' own lifetime, scholastics may have been questioning the relevance of what they were asked to study. His answer, with its appeal to charity and obedience, and its side-stepping of the issue of relevance, would not prove persuasive today. It seems like a defensive response or at best a rhetorical one. However, it should not be taken as contradicting his more basic principle that studies are meant to be instrumental in our co-operation with God in God's plan of salvation. This is again stated in the letter to Brandão:

> In addition, one can practice frequently offering to God our Lord his studies along with the effort that these demand, keeping in mind that we undertake them for his love and setting aside our personal tastes so as to render some service to his Divine Majesty by helping those for whose life he died.[31]

---

[31] Ignatius, *Letters*, 342.

Whatever is dominant in a person's life at any particular time is that person's main access to God. For scholastics it will be their studies, and there is no point in trying to find God apart from these. Commitment to study is how these young men will find God, and devotion comes from the offering of their labour to the God who is labouring for them—precisely in those same studies.

In writing to, or about, scholastics in studies, Ignatius draws on his own experience as a student. While at the University of Paris he had lost the regular consolations that he had enjoyed in Spain. These only returned when his studies ended.[32] Does this mean that he had no devotion in Paris—that he was not easily finding God there? Similarly, if the scholastics find that there is no affective resonance in their prayer or in their life of study, are they too bereft of devotion? Ignatius deals with this subtle question in a letter to Bartolomé Hernández where he distinguishes between *devoción* and *gusto de devoción* (devotion and the 'relish' of devotion).

> It is no cause for wonder that not all of our own students experience the relish of devotion [*gusto de devoción*] that one might desire. He who dispenses this grace does so when and where he thinks fit. During the time of studies, which impose considerable spiritual effort, we may presume that divine Wisdom sometimes suspends sensible visitations of this sort, for although they give great delight to the spirit, they sometimes excessively weaken the body. Moreover, the occupation of the mind with academic pursuits naturally tends to produce a certain dryness in the interior affections.[33]

Does the dryness to which Ignatius here refers owe more to the kinds of philosophy and theology then being studied and to their methodology than to study in itself? Scholastic philosophy and theology had become so cerebral and academic since the fourteenth century that it is difficult to see how they could nourish

---

[32] 'During the period that he was in Vicenza, he received many spiritual visions and many rather ordinary consolations (it was just the opposite when he was in Paris), but especially when he began to prepare for his ordination in Venice and when he was getting ready to celebrate Mass.' (*Autobiography*, n. 95)

[33] Ignatius to Bartolomé Hernández, 21 July 1554, Ignatius, *Letters*, 494–495, here 494. The recipient was rector of a newly founded college in Salamanca.

a person's affectivity. A more experientially based philosophy and a more pastorally orientated theology (such as the Renaissance humanists proposed, and such as are widely offered today) can engage the whole person. They can actually be a stimulus to the reception of affective graces, those 'sensible visitations' as Ignatius calls them.

Nevertheless, the distinction between an essential devotion (strongly associated with purity of intention) and an affective resonance remains valid. Even if it is not study that leads to dryness, other situations and engagements can do so. The experience of living in contemporary secularised society can itself have this effect. A person who relies on *gusto de devoción* as a measure of his or her commitment, or even faith, is building on sand.

4.

THE LONGED-FOR SENDING

THE PRIMARY SIGNIFICANCE of the word 'mission', at least from an Ignatian point of view, is as a verb rather than as a noun. It has the active meaning of 'to send' or the passive meaning of 'to be sent'. Only secondarily does it signify a content, 'the work one is sent to do', or 'the mission that one is given'. For the sake of clarity it may be better to confine the word 'mission' to its primary meaning as a verb, and to use some word such as 'ministry' or 'service' to indicate the task or project ('mission' in its secondary sense) with which one has been entrusted. But even if one does use the word 'mission' for the content or the work, it is always understood that one undertakes this work only because one has been sent to do so.[1]

Mission as a Surrender to God

This points to a very important insight: that mission is a living out of an attitude of surrender and abandonment of ourselves to God, an attitude expressed so powerfully in the prayer, 'Take, Lord, and receive!' Mission, therefore, implies that we are no longer in control of our own life, but that someone else disposes of it. This is not an alien imposition but the result of a choice made by us in freedom under grace. 'All of it is yours. Dispose of it according to your will. Give me love of yourself along with your grace, for that is enough for me.' (Exx 234) This offering is the final form in which indifference, or interior freedom, is expressed in the Spiritual Exercises. It began as a 'freedom from' sin, disorder, selfishness (and the baleful influence of the 'world') but soon grew into a 'freedom for' discipleship, service, ministry (all in an ecclesial context).

In the Spiritual Exercises the turning point from one kind of freedom to the other is in the Call of the King (Exx 91–98). Here

---

[1] The meaning of 'mission' in Ignatius' usage is discussed by Antonio M. de Aldama in *The Constitutions of the Society of Jesus, Part VII: Missioning*, translated by Ignacio Echániz (Rome: CIS, 1990), 7–12. See also John W. O'Malley, 'Mission and the Early Jesuits', *The Way Supplement*, 79 (Spring 1994), 3–10.

the two inseparable elements of discipleship, close companionship with Christ and collaboration in his project (both expressed by the word *conmigo*) are put before the exercitant. They are then meant to develop, deepen and become more specific in form throughout the rest of the Exercises, culminating in the process of election and in the unitive prayer of the Third and Fourth Weeks. The paradox is that the call from Jesus to 'Come, follow me', and the call to 'Go, make disciples of all nations' are one and the same call.[2] This understanding will be presupposed in the *Constitutions*.

The Role of Imagination

Ignatius' own motivation and drive did not so much come from an exegetical reading of the scriptures as from a series of images, pictures, scenes that fascinated him imaginatively. We know from his own account of his conversion at Loyola in the *Autobiography* that he had the capacity to be captivated for hours by stories, personalities and events, some fictional, others historical (nn. 5–10). It was his imagination as much as, if not more than, his reason that led him to commit his life totally to Christ.[3]

As he matured spiritually, and as he became less focused on asceticism and more on his desire 'to help souls', the memory or image that drew Ignatius like a magnet (as it had drawn Francis and Dominic before him) was that of Jesus sending apostles and disciples on missionary journeys. So the *Constitutions* will describe the intention of the First Companions as,

> ... to travel throughout the world and, when they could not find the desired spiritual fruit in one place, to pass on to another and another, ever seeking the greater glory of God our Lord and the greater aid of souls (VII. 1. B [605]).[4]

---

[2] To respond only to the 'Come' risks the emergence of a narcissistic or individualistic spirituality. To respond only to the 'Go' risks issuing in a driven activism, losing touch with its contemplative roots. It may well end in burnout. Both Ignatius and the Gospels before him were more holistic in approach.

[3] See Brian O'Leary, 'Spirituality and Imagination', *Spirituality*, 9 (2003), 165–168.

[4] It is no wonder that Ignatius in the *Autobiography* always refers to himself as 'the pilgrim', although the earlier pilgrimage for penitential purposes gradually evolves into

As background to this text, and to the whole of part VII of the *Constitutions*, we might briefly recall three references in the Exercises to apostolic journeys, undertaken either by Christ or (when sent) by his followers.

The first is the composition of place for the meditation on the Call of the King, where Ignatius sets before the exercitant 'the synagogues, villages, and castles through which Christ our Lord passed as he preached' (Exx 91). This is an obvious allusion to Matthew 9:35, 'Then Jesus went about all the cities and villages, teaching in their synagogues, and proclaiming the good news of the kingdom, and curing every disease and every sickness'.[5] Secondly, in the meditation on the Two Standards, this invitation is put before the exercitant:

> Consider the address which Christ our Lord makes to all his servants and friends whom he is sending on this expedition. He recommends that they endeavour to aid all persons ....
> (Exx 146)

Finally, among the mysteries of Christ's life suggested for contemplation, Ignatius outlines one entitled 'How the Apostles Were Sent To Preach'. Its three points give a summary of chapter 10 of Matthew's Gospel (Exx 281). In their varied ways these three texts concern mission, both in its primary meaning of 'a sending', and in its secondary meaning of a commission, a mandate or a charge. (Jesus considered himself as having been sent by the Father, as we shall see below.)

The dominant place in Ignatius' imaginative memory of Jesus and his followers being constantly 'on the road' is further underlined in the teaching of Nadal. Some quotations from

---

the pilgrimage for apostolic goals. Yet the image of the pilgrimage, the journey, the road remains constant. See John Olin, 'The Idea of Pilgrimage in the Experience of Ignatius Loyola', *Church History*, 48 (1979), 387–397, and Mario Scaduto, 'La strada e i primi gesuiti', *AHSI*, 40 (1971), 323–390.

[5] This emphasis on movement is particularly clear in an episode in Mark. Simon and his companions have come to Jesus with the news that in Capernaum, 'Everyone is searching for you', clearly expecting him to return there. But Jesus replies, 'Let us go on to the neighbouring towns, so that I may proclaim the message there also; for that is what I came out to do' (Mark 1:37–38). The imperative to keep pushing forward is similar to that in *Constitutions* VII.1.B[605].

his writings have become well known in recent years.[6] For example:

> It must be noted that in the Society there are different kinds of houses or dwellings. These are: the house of probation, the college, the professed house, and the journey—and by this last the whole world becomes our house.[7]

> For wherever they can be sent in ministry to bring aid to souls, that is the most glorious and longed-for 'house' for these theologians .... They realise that they cannot build or acquire enough houses to be able from nearby to run out to the combat. Since that is the case, they consider that they are in their most peaceful and pleasant house when they are constantly on the move, when they travel throughout the earth, when they have no place to call their own, when they are always in need, always in want—only let them strive in some small way to imitate Christ Jesus who had nowhere on which to lay his head and who spent all his years of preaching in journey.[8]

The link with the Exercises is clear in another text in which Nadal is commenting on the commitment required by the Fourth Vow:

> This is a work that is at the same time of the greatest difficulty, labour, and danger, as well as the greatest utility and necessity. It is hence that the Society seems somehow to imitate the condition of the Church of the Apostles, in our humility in Christ.[9]

Nadal here points implicitly to the Third Way of Being Humble, as well as to the wider themes of discipleship and service that permeate the Second Week. He is fascinated by the idea of Jesuits being apostles and, as a body, recreating the primitive Church. Elsewhere he writes:

---

[6] Influential in bringing these texts to our notice has been John W. O'Malley, 'To Travel to Any Part of the World: Jerónimo Nadal and the Jesuit Vocation', *Studies in the Spirituality of Jesuits*, 16/2 (1984). I use his English translations of Nadal from this work.

[7] MHSJ MN 5, 54.

[8] MHSJ MN 5, 773.

[9] MHSJ MN 5, 196.

> Our vocation is similar to the vocation and training of the Apostles: first, we come to know the Society, and then we follow; we are instructed; we receive our commission to be sent; we are sent; we exercise our ministry; we are prepared to die for Christ in fulfilling those ministries.[10]

O'Malley comments:

> Nadal does not use the term 'Apostles' and 'apostolic' in a casual sense simply to indicate ministries, but with the understanding that in his day the Society was recovering an aspect of the primitive Church that was especially its own.[11]

Mystical Experiences

But let us return to Ignatius. While the starting point for his understanding of mission was the simple gospel scene of Jesus' sending of his apostles and disciples, his mystical experience brought him much more deeply into the mystery. In his *Spiritual Diary*, the entry for 11 February 1544[12] contains this statement:

> … and at the same moment I received new insights, viz. that the Son first sent his Apostles to preach in poverty, and later the Holy Spirit, by granting his spirit and his gift of tongues, confirmed them, and thus, since both Father and Son sent the Holy Spirit, all three Persons confirmed such a mission.[13]

Here we find ourselves, not just with the human Jesus of the Gospels, but being drawn into the life, relationships and activity of the Trinitarian God. The apostolic mission or sending of the apostles by Jesus (and by implication the sending of others from later generations in the name of Jesus) is pondered under four aspects:

[10] Nadal, *Orationis observationes*, MHSJ MN 6, 138.
[11] O'Malley, 'To Travel to Any Part of the World', 7. For a further development of the 'apostolic' self-understanding of the first Jesuits see 'In Imitation of Jesus and the Primitive Church', chapter 6 in Joseph F. Conwell, *Walking in the Spirit: A Reflection on Jerónimo Nadal's Phrase 'Contemplative Likewise in Action'* (St Louis: Institute of Jesuit Sources, 2003), 71–99.
[12] De Aldama, *Missioning*, 8, points out that this is hardly a month before Ignatius began to write the preparatory text known as *Constitutiones circa missiones*.
[13] *Spiritual Diary*, 76. Note the recurrence here in 1544 of the phrase 'to preach in poverty', first found in his 1536 letter to Cassador.

- the historical sending of the apostles by Jesus during his public ministry;

- the confirmation of this sending by the Holy Spirit through his gift to those sent (a) of his own spirit working interiorly in their lives, and (b) of the external manifestation of the word (symbolized by the gift of tongues);

- the further confirmation of this sending by all Three Divine Persons;

- both the sending by Jesus (the Son) and the confirmation given by the Holy Spirit are the extension *ad extra* (that is, into the created world) of the inner relationships of the Trinity. In other words, the missioning by Jesus of the apostles is an incarnational extension of the *spiratio* or breathing by which the Father and the Son eternally 'send' the Holy Spirit.[14]

This text shows how central 'sending' is in the Ignatian scheme of things. It also alerts us to approach part VII of the *Constitutions* (on the missioning or sending of members), not just as a masterpiece of effective person management within the corporate venture that is the Society of Jesus, but even more as a concrete, incarnational expression of Ignatius' mystical intuition.

These insights, recorded by Ignatius in his *Spiritual Diary* in 1544, were not in essence totally new, although they added a greater theological clarity and depth to his understanding of mission. Already at Manresa he had enjoyed an intellectual vision of the Trinity, and on the banks of the Cardoner he had received the 'great illumination', as a result of which he saw all things as new (*Autobiography*, nn. 28–30). It was in the light of the consolation brought to him by these experiences that his apostolic spirituality had begun to take on a recognisable and consistent shape. This apostolic thrust of his spirituality cannot be divorced from the mystical experiences themselves.[15]

---

[14] With slight adaptations I follow the interpretation found in de Aldama, *Missioning*, 8–9. The author cites with approval the comments of Peter Knauer in *Ignatius von Loyola: das geistliche Tagebuch*, edited by Adolf Haas and Peter Knauer (Freiburg: Herder, 1961), 250 n. 3.

[15] See chapter 1.

There is continuity, therefore, between 1522–1523 at Manresa and 1544 in Rome. In between, in 1537, came the vision at La Storta. On his way to Rome with Favre and Laínez (as we saw in chapter 1), while praying in a small ruined chapel in the village of La Storta, almost within sight of Rome, Ignatius saw clearly 'God the Father place him with Christ, his Son' (*Autobiography*, n.96). He had been praying throughout the journey to Mary for precisely this grace, but when it was given, Ignatius intuitively knew that it was not destined for him alone. His interpretation of the experience was that Christ was admitting the whole group of the early companions into his service. One might say that he felt and understood (*sentir*) something of the mystical dimension of the apostolic companionship that was to be theirs. This apostolic companionship was to be their community, and through this they would be drawn into the community of the Trinity.

Johannine Insights[16]

An Ignatian understanding of mission, as indeed any Christian understanding of mission, has to be christological, and ultimately Trinitarian. For Jesus in his humanity the Father meant everything. The favour of the Father was the air he breathed, and the will of the Father was the food on which he lived. Time and again, particularly in the Gospel of John, we see the profound fascination that the Father exercised on the human sensibility of Jesus. His personal sense of identity, as well as the human choices he made throughout his life, came from his experience of a profound filial relationship with the Father. His mission appears, therefore, not so much as coming to him from 'outside' himself, but as being an intrinsic part of who he is. His identity and his mission are one. *To be Son is to be sent, is to be on mission.*

---

[16] The common approach to Ignatian spirituality tends to find more support in the synoptic Gospels than in that of John. So it is interesting to discover Hans Urs von Balthasar writing, 'For John, the revelation of God in Christ is the Incarnation of the Word in this One, who is unique, loved and adored. Ignatius appears to me as the point in history where the encounter of man with the God who is the Word and has the word, who addresses, chooses and calls, has become inescapable. In my view, all that is decisive takes place in the spiritual space that lies between the two poles of John and Ignatius.' (*My Work: In Retrospect* [San Francisco: Ignatius, 1993], 20)

We might allow the cumulative effect of these texts from the Gospel of John, all of them containing the verb 'to send', to convey something of this reality to us:

> My food is to do the will of him who sent me and to complete his work (4:34).

> I can do nothing on my own. As I hear, I judge; and my judgment is just, because I seek to do not my own will but the will of him who sent me. (5:30)

> I have come down from heaven, not to do my own will, but the will of him who sent me (6:38).

> I judge no one. Yet even if I judge, my judgment is valid; for it is not I alone who judge, but I and the Father who sent me. (8:15–16)

> When you have lifted up the Son of Man, then you will realise that I am he, and that I do nothing on my own, but I speak these things as the Father instructed me. And the one who sent me is with me; he has not left me alone, for I always do what is pleasing to him. (8:28–29)

As with Jesus, so with us—as baptized, as Jesuits, as the body of the Society. We share in Christ's mission because, and in so far as, we share in his Sonship. For us also *to be sons* is *to be sent* is *to be on mission.*

But what of love? The word does not occur in any of the above quotations. Yet it is the ultimate source and driving force of the mission of Jesus and of his followers.[17] Mission may be said to sacramentalise God's love (and ours), to make it present and effective in a tangible way. Consider side by side these two other Johannine texts:

> As the Father has loved me, so have I loved you (15:9).

> As the Father has sent me, even so I send you (20:21).

---

[17] 'We must not be fooled by [Jesus'] language in the Gospel of John to the effect that he only does what the Father commands. These statements mean that he received everything he was from God the Source and that he "returned" everything to the Source out of grateful love.' (John B. Foley, 'Stepping into the River: Reflections on the Vows', *Studies in the Spirituality of Jesuits*, 26/4 [1994], 20) Here Foley points to the mutuality of the Contemplation to Attain the Love of God.

This is more than a rhetorical parallelism. The loving and being loved, the sending and being sent, are ultimately one reality.

Constitutions: Part VII

Of the 23 occurrences of the word 'mission' in the *Constitutions*, seventeen appear in part VII. We are already aware of how this part forms the core or pivot of the *Constitutions*. Everything that precedes it, in the General Examen and in parts I to VI, deals with the developmental process by which a person is incorporated into the body of the Society and, simultaneously, is brought to a state of availability, preparedness and zeal for dispersal on mission. The later parts VIII, IX and X will look to the necessary corporate supports for that mission. These will consist of union of minds and hearts, effective spiritual governance, and the preservation and increase of the body and the spirit of the Society.

If we take an alternative (or perhaps complementary) approach to the text, viewing the *Constitutions* as 'a spirit in search of a body', then in part VII we find that body being articulated in the very dispersal of the members on mission. The body is not fully itself, it has not reached its optimum organic growth, until its members are dispersed on mission. The spirit is most fully incarnated when the body is in dispersal.[18]

Historically speaking, the imperative of dispersal for mission was acknowledged and accepted by the early companions a significant time before they came to see the necessity of 'forming themselves into one body'. Furthermore, even if in 1539 they had decided against forming themselves into one body and vowing 'to obey one of us', they would still have given themselves to a life of dispersal for mission. This is apparent in the opening sentences of the *Deliberation of the First Fathers*:

> Near the end of Lent the time was drawing near when we would have to be dispersed and separated from one another. We were very eager for this, recognising it as necessary in order to reach the goal we had already fixed upon and thought about with intense desire. (n. 1)

[18] These two approaches to the *Constitutions* were touched on towards the end of chapter 1.

As they began their Deliberation, the companions as a group had no definite preconception about founding a religious order. That was only one among many possibilities. But they were quite certain and assured about their vocation to universal priestly ministry, and about the inevitable link between that calling and dispersal.[19]

Constitutiones circa missiones

Against such a background it is no surprise to find that part VII is the oldest section of the *Constitutions*, around which the other parts eventually took shape.[20] The earliest preparatory documents, written by Ignatius around 1544–1545, are entitled *Constitutiones circa missiones* and *Declarationes circa missiones*, that is, some Constitutions and their corresponding Declarations (or clarifications) concerning missions.[21]

These early documents are naturally not as well known as the definitive *Constitutions*, so it is enlightening to discover what they say. They show us in a concise form Ignatius' initial approach to the choice and ordering of topics that would eventually become the content of part VII. The *Constitutiones circa missiones* are divided into six chapters:

1. This describes the origin of the Fourth Vow and its purpose: '... that His Holiness might oversee our dispersal or mission for the greater glory of God our Lord, in conformity with our promise and intent of going through the whole world'.

2. This prohibits any Jesuit from seeking 'mediately or immediately' to stay in, or go to, any particular place.

3. This outlines the offering of availability that every Jesuit must make of himself to the Pope, especially in regard to material arrangements for his journey.

4. This recommends that one who is being sent, before setting out, should receive written instructions regarding his mission.

---

[19] The Deliberation was discussed in chapter 1 under the heading 'Two Pivotal Choices'.
[20] A note in his *Spiritual Diary* for 17 March 1544 reads: 'Here I began my preparation and first consideration concerning the missions' (*Spiritual Diary*, 101).
[21] MHSJ Const. 1, 159–164.

5. This underlines the mobility that is proper to the Jesuit who should not, in general, be involved longer than three months with any particular mission.

6. This proposes that, within a year following the election of a new Pope, the Superior General should present to him the 'profession, obedience and promise made by the Society'.

The *Declarationes circa missiones* contain five paragraphs:

1. Further reference is made to the authority of the Superior General to send Jesuits to Christian countries.[22]

2. This insists on the universalism of outlook which the Superior General must retain in sending Jesuits on missions. An initial attempt to indicate criteria for sending.

3. The meaning of a Jesuit's indifference with regard to his mission is clarified. He may not scheme but may reveal his inner movements to his superior.

4. This clarifies the source of the instructions that a Jesuit should receive in setting out on a mission.

5. A practical recommendation is made concerning letter writing.

As we consider the evolution of the *Constitutions* through these early documents to their final form, a useful parallel can be kept in mind. Just as the New Testament grew out of, and was an expression of, the lived experience of the primitive Church and did not originate that experience, so the *Constitutions* grew out of, and expressed, the lived experience of the primitive Society and did not originate that experience. Throughout the sixteen years from the papal approbation of the Society in 1540 to the death of Ignatius in 1556, the *Constitutions* evolved in large part by mirroring the life, and especially the apostolic experience, of Jesuits over an increasingly large part of the world.

Hence arose one reason for the insistence of Ignatius on regular correspondence between the dispersed Jesuits and Rome.[23]

---

[22] This paragraph contains the important description of the Fourth Vow as *nuestro principio y principal fundamento* ('our starting point and principal foundation'). The phrase has obvious resonances with the Principle and Foundation in the Spiritual Exercises.

[23] Other reasons were an aid to union of minds and hearts (*Constitutions* VIII. 1.9–N[673–676]), and an aid to governance. These will be discussed in chapter 5.

Of course there was the immediate need to guide his men in their current situations and difficulties. But Ignatius also wanted feedback from those ministering in the vineyard of the Lord so that he could discern and incorporate this experience into the *Constitutions*. Similarly, when he sent Nadal to various provinces to promulgate the *Constitutions* he wanted Nadal's opinion as to whether this document corresponded with what was happening on the ground.[24] Hence, too, Ignatius desired to leave the *Constitutions* open-ended so that they would continue to respond to changing situations and needs. In a way the *Constitutions* legitimised what was already happening rather than attempting to make things happen.[25]

Development of Part VII

Part VII is a good example of this mode of development. To take just one issue: The *Constitutiones circa missiones* and the *Declarationes circa missiones* present a picture of the Society and its members in almost ceaseless movement. There is no mention in these documents (1544–1545) of any established residence for Jesuits, or of what we would call a local community. But by 1550, when text *a* of the Constitutions was ready, the existence of a stable domicile was taken for granted. This would remain the case in all further redactions of the text. Nevertheless, through all of these changes Ignatius never loses sight of the primary meaning of 'mission' as a sending.

The title of part VII reads, 'The relations to their neighbour of those already incorporated into the Society when they are dispersed into the vineyard of Christ our Lord'. How are they dispersed? The opening paragraph summarises the four ways in which the members can be sent:

---

[24] Ignatius showed his implicit trust in Nadal when he said, on sending him to promulgate and explain the *Constitutions* throughout Europe, 'He altogether knows my mind and enjoys the same authority as myself' (MHSJ MN 1, 144). Similar sentiments are echoed in Polanco's words to Diego Miró, 'Nadal understands well the mind of our Father Ignatius, for he has dealt with him extensively, and seems to have grasped his spirit, and has penetrated the Institute as thoroughly as anyone I know in the Society' (MHSJ EI 5, 109).
[25] Of course, once the *Constitutions* were promulgated, and especially after the First General Congregation in 1558 approved them, they became a formative influence on the life of the Society. Again, this parallels the history of the New Testament.

- '... whether they have been sent to some places or others by either the supreme vicar of Christ our Lord';

- 'or the superiors of the Society, who for them are similarly in the place of his Divine Majesty';

- 'or whether they themselves choose where and in what work they will labour, having been commissioned to travel to any place where they judge that greater service of God and the good of souls will follow';

- 'or whether they carry on their labour not by travelling but by residing steadily and continually in certain places where much fruit of glory and service to God is expected' (VII. 1. 1 [603]).

This sequence of four ways of being sent follows the changing pattern of the mode of distribution of the companions from 1539 to 1550. Its roots are thus partly historical. In turn it corresponds to the four chapters that make up part VII. The order does not claim to prioritise ways of being sent but rather underscores the variety of possible concrete insertions into the common Jesuit experience of mission. The members, now fully incorporated into the body of the Society, face the challenge of being incorporated into the world, the Lord's vineyard. In Ignatius' view this requires a 'sending'.[26]

Although chapter 4, on 'Ways in which the houses and colleges can help their neighbours', goes into some detail, the main thrust of part VII is not about the 'content' of missions but how they are to be initiated. This is partly because the Society's ways of helping souls are already established in the *Formula of the Institute* (1550) and do not need further elaboration.

> He is a member of a Society founded chiefly for this purpose: to strive especially for the defence and propagation of the faith and for the progress of souls in Christian life and doctrine, by means of public preaching, lectures, and any other ministration

---

[26] It is in part VII that Ignatian obedience reaches its deepest maturity and meaning as the member's free and willing response to being 'sent'. The earlier ascetical and mystical emphases (General Examen, parts III and VI) are not abandoned or abrogated, but are subsumed into the core Jesuit experience of obedience for mission.

whatsoever of the word of God, and further by means of the Spiritual Exercises, the education of children and unlettered persons in Christianity, and the spiritual consolation of Christ's faithful through hearing confessions and administering the other sacraments. Moreover, he should show himself ready to reconcile the estranged, compassionately assist and serve those who are in prisons or hospitals, and indeed to perform any other works of charity, according to what will seem expedient for the glory of God and the common good. (n. 1)

Here we find a variety of ministries and apostolic initiatives brought together in three clusters. They are sometimes named as (a) ministries of the word; (b) ministries of the spirit; and (c) ministries of charity or mercy. These designations are perhaps the most straightforward. But there is an alternative, more subtle, approach. It is based on a conviction that the fundamental, all-embracing Jesuit ministry is that of the word. From this perspective the Formula is dividing Jesuit apostolic engagements into (a) ministries that proclaim the word; (b) ministries that interiorise the word; and (c) ministries that express the word through compassionate action (witness). This latter interpretation, which is persuasive, offers us an important clue towards an understanding of Jesuit priesthood. It points to this priesthood as primarily (but not exclusively) a priesthood of the word, a prophetic priesthood, in contrast to a more cultic or sacramental model to which others are rightly called.[27]

Discernment of Ministries

The Formula, therefore, tells Jesuits in a general way what to do when they are sent, and this 'work' will be further specified in each case by the one who sends. However, part VII is more focused on the process of sending. Ignatius' personal offering of

---

[27] Such a contrast can be overstated in a way that almost subsumes the ministerial priesthood in the general priesthood of all the faithful. This can happen out of a misconceived desire to eliminate all differences between ordained Jesuits and Jesuit brothers, or from a false sensitivity towards lay collaborators. Religious brothers and laity can and do exercise a ministry of the word. But the cultic or sacramental dimension is as essential a component of Jesuit priesthood as of that of other priests, even if not the primary one. See reading references on Jesuit priesthood in chapter 2.

himself to the Pope in 1538, subsequently made juridical by the Fourth Vow, presumed that the Pope would be the one who sent. However, circumstances changed rapidly as the Society's numbers grew and as requests for Jesuit ministries multiplied. In 1542 Ignatius secured permission (as Superior General) to send Jesuits to Christian countries,[28] and in 1549 to send Jesuits to any place whatever, even among the 'infidels' or non-believers.[29] In light of these developments, Ignatius was very conscious that the Society's superiors general would need help in this crucial area of discernment: the sending of Jesuits in the most apostolically effective manner. In chapter 2 he deals with the issues of where to send (VII. 2. D [622]), the purpose for which to send (VII. 2. E [623]), whom to send and how many (VII. 2. F [624]), how to send (VII. 2. G [625]) and for how long (VII. 2. H [626]).[30]

The purpose of all this detail is well expressed in the text that reads:

> Hence, the superior general, or whoever holds this authority from him, ought to bestow much careful thought on missions of this kind, so that, in sending subjects to one region rather than to another, or for one purpose rather than for another, or one particular person rather than another or several of them, in this manner or in that, or for a longer or shorter time, that may always be done which is conducive to the greater service of God and the universal good (VII. 2. 1 [618]).

Ignatius is asking that a process of discernment, analogous to the election in the Spiritual Exercises, precede every sending of a Jesuit, every 'mission'. Such is 'our way of proceeding' that must always be in place as a necessary component of spiritual governance. It is a process built on indifference or that 'thoroughly right and pure intention in the presence of God our Lord' (VII. 2. 1 [618]). It presupposes a common apostolic vision and desire shared by the superior (the one sending) and the individual

---

[28] This faculty was granted orally by Paul III at the request of Cardinal Guidiccioni.
[29] The Bull *Licet debitum* of Paul III included this extension of the Superior General's right to send.
[30] See Joseph Veale, 'Ignatian Criteria for Choice of Ministries', in *Manifold Gifts*, 109–122. I am indebted to this article in what follows.

Jesuit (the one being sent). Each has his contribution to make, through prayer and dialogue, in order that the discernment may lead to a good decision.

In this discernment process, missioning brings together the interactive realities of the divine and the human.[31] The underpinning of the entire process is not some merely human insight or natural intelligence, but the wisdom that comes from a lived faith and spiritual sensitivity.

> Although it is the supreme providence and direction of the Holy Spirit that must efficaciously bring us to make the right decision in all matters, and to send to each place those who are best fitted and suited to the people and tasks for which they are sent .... (VII.2.F[624])

But when this faith foundation has been laid, and its requirements accepted, then human reasoning, understanding, imagination, experience and creativity come into play, as the many lists of criteria offered by Ignatius make clear. The discernment that is missioning is a co-operative venture, most obviously between the one who sends and the one being sent, but at a deeper level between God and God's human instruments. God, as always, respects human freedom and the laws of God's own creation by working through human potential and human limitation. Ultimately mission is mystery, a sharing in the mystery of Christ's incarnation and, as we reflected earlier, an experience of being drawn into the life and the love of the Trinitarian community.

Criteria for Choice

The criteria presented by Ignatius in chapter 2 are many and detailed, and their interrelationships are complex. It would be impossible to examine them all here. Instead we shall confine our attention to just one set of criteria, those offered to help with the question 'where to send?' Although the issue is posed in terms of place, it could equally well be formulated in terms of

---

[31] See my discussion of this polarity in chapter 7.

persons ('to whom to send?'), since all apostolic involvement is essentially interpersonal. In any case, the specific criteria are introduced by an overarching principle:

> To make the best choice in sending persons to one place or another while having the greater service of God and the more universal good before one's eyes as the guiding norm ....
> (VII.2.D[622])

Immediately we recognise the *magis* of the Principle and Foundation appearing in the phrases 'the greater service' and 'the more universal good'. There is also a clear indication that those involved in the process must look towards God and keep their eyes on God. Hence this use of suggested criteria is to be a contemplative exercise. We are reminded of the words from the *Formula*: 'Still further, let any such person take care, as long as he lives, first of all to keep before his eyes God ...' (n.3).

Then comes the first specific criterion:

> ... it would appear that in the ample vineyard of the Lord one ought to select, other things being equal (and this should be understood in everything that follows), that part of the vineyard which has greater need, both because of lack of other workers, and because of the wretchedness and infirmity of the people there and their danger of eternal condemnation (VII.2.D[622]).

Ignatius sees two reasons for considering a situation as a greater need. These are the 'lack of other workers' and 'the wretchedness and infirmity' of the people there. This latter misery and weakness is primarily of the moral and spiritual kind, as the reference to eternal condemnation indicates. What he has in mind appears vividly in one of his letters:

> See your neighbours also—images of the Most Holy Trinity, capable of possessing the glory of him whom the whole universe serves, members of Jesus Christ redeemed by him with so much pain, opprobrium, and blood—see how wretched is their state, in such deep darkness of ignorance and amid such storms of desires, vain fears, and other passions; assailed by so many visible and invisible enemies; in danger of losing, not their property or temporal life, but the kingdom and

eternal happiness, and of falling into the unbearable misery of everlasting fire.[32]

We recognise in Ignatius' letter a sensitivity to the particular needs crying out to be met and a deep desire to meet them. He interprets what he sees in theological terms, in the light of Christian belief. This leads him to emphasize the stark alternatives that people are facing between 'the kingdom and eternal happiness' and 'the unbearable misery of everlasting fire'. As in VII.2.D[622], the spiritual danger of damnation outweighs that of temporal suffering or need.[33]

Nadal, in his talks and writings, made much of the criterion of the greater need. For example:

> This is indeed the distinctive mark of our vocation: that we accept from God and the orthodox Church the care of those for whom nobody is caring, even if there actually is somebody who ought to be caring for them. And if there is nobody else, surely the supreme Vicar of Christ, the Roman Pontiff [has them in his care]. To him, therefore, we are given in service, that through us he might care for those for whom their ordinaries or priests are of no avail, or especially those who altogether lack an ordinary. To this end looks our vow that is made to the Supreme Pontiff, which specifically concerns 'missions'. This is a work that is at the same time of the greatest difficulty, labour and danger, as well as the greatest utility and necessity. It is hence that the Society seems somehow to imitate the condition of the Church of the Apostles, in our humility in Christ.[34]

De Aldama questions whether Nadal's notable stress on this particular criterion is fully in line with the mind of Ignatius. He

---

[32] Ignatius to the Fathers and Scholastics at Coimbra, 7 May 1547, known as 'The Letter of Perfection', Ignatius, *Letters*, 166–174, here 170.
[33] Ignatius did not have the tools of social and cultural analysis that are available to us today, nor the means of mass media communication that can broaden and deepen our understanding of the world and its needs. Theology too has developed, and the fear of people's eternal damnation, which so drove the First Companions, would not be shared by most contemporary Jesuits. The rhetoric around 'faith and justice' is an indication of yet another theological shift. Even a document such as *Gaudium et spes* of Vatican II shows the growth in historical consciousness and social awareness between the sixteenth and mid-twentieth centuries.
[34] MHSJ MN 5, 195–196.

argues: 'It is neither the only one [criterion] nor the main one, if we keep in mind Ignatius' other writings'.[35] Whether this judgment is correct or not, the criterion of 'the greater need' has remained a powerful influence and stimulus to Jesuit decision making up to our own day.

The theme of the *magis* is continued in the other four criteria for 'where to send?' The second states that:

> Consideration should also be given to where greater fruit is likely to be reaped through the means usual in the Society (VII. 2. D [622]).

These means were well established in the Formula and were not in dispute. Signs that reaping the desired greater fruit was probable include 'where one sees the door more widely open and a better disposition and readiness among the people to be profited'. In developing this point Ignatius speaks of 'their greater devotion and desire' in a way that is similar to his thinking in Annotation 20 of the Spiritual Exercises. Just as he wants the full Exercises to be given only to 'a person who is more disengaged, and who desires to make all the progress possible',[36] so he is looking to send Jesuits to those 'who are more capable of making progress and of preserving the fruit produced to the glory of God our Lord'.

The third criterion is that of a greater debt of gratitude. In Ignatius' day professed houses were supported by alms, and colleges were in large part dependent on endowments provided by rich benefactors. A place where such generosity was being experienced had a greater claim on the Society's ministries than other locations, 'assuming that the other considerations pertaining to spiritual progress are equal'. This criterion was never meant to be the overriding one. Today, given the changed socio-economic situation of most Jesuit ministries, as well as the need to maintain an apostolic freedom of speech and action, the criterion of greater debt is increasingly problematic and possibly irrelevant. Our debt of gratitude to benefactors can be expressed in other ways

---

[35] De Aldama, *Missioning*, 75. He suggests that 'greater fruit' may be the main criterion, but adds, *'ceteris paribus*, of course'.
[36] See also *Constitutions* IV. 8. E [409], VII. 4. F [649].

that do not risk compromising our integrity or the prophetic dimension of our ministries.

The fourth criterion is more significant, and the text begins with a restatement of the principle of universality: 'The more universal the good is, the more is it divine'. It continues:

> Hence preference ought to be given to persons and places which, once benefited themselves, are a cause of extending the good to many others who are under their influence or take guidance from them (VII. 2. D [622]).

In contemporary terminology the goal here is a greater multiplying effect. For Ignatius the persons who influence and guide many others are 'important and public persons' who wield authority and are held in esteem, either for their own worth, or for the social position that they occupy, or for the role that they play in public administration. When Diego Miró and later Gonçalves da Câmara were asked to be confessors at the court of King John III of Portugal they demurred. When Ignatius heard this he wrote instructing them to accept the post. He said that they had not made the right decision originally, and then gave a number of reasons including the following:

> Then, if we look to the universal good and God's greater service, these will, so far as I can perceive in the Lord, ensue more strongly from this. For the good of the head is shared by all the body's members, and the good of the sovereign by all his subjects, so that spiritual benefit given to the sovereign should be rated above that which might be given to others.[37]

The late medieval world-view of Ignatius, with its hierarchical understanding of society, is obvious in this text. The principle that 'the good of the head is shared by all the body's members' will reappear in the context of the Society and its Superior

---

[37] Ignatius to Diego Miró, 1 February 1553, Ignatius, *Letters*, 410–411, here 410. De Aldama supplements this example: 'He [Ignatius] wrote in the same vein to Laínez a few months later, telling him to return to Florence; the reason was that he valued more one degree of spiritual benefit in the person and household of the Duchess than many degrees in others, "because the good accomplished in her soul can spread a good deal to the universal good"' (*Missioning*, 79, citing MHSJ EI 5, 649).

General.[38] Yet in spite of the difference between this mindset and that of a democratic and more egalitarian society, the principle of the greater multiplying effect is still valid. There are always people who, either because of their own worth or the position and authority they hold, have a much wider influence than others do. There are those on the national or world stage whose opinions are respected, whose lifestyle is imitated, who become role models (especially for the young). If such people are evangelized and openly live by the gospel message, many others will be reached and drawn to Christ.

The fifth and last criterion is unexpected:

> Similarly, in places where the enemy of Christ our Lord is seen to have sown cockle (Matthew 13:24–30), particularly where he has spread bad opinion about the Society or stirred up ill will against it so as to impede the fruit which it might produce, the Society ought to exert itself more, especially if it is an important place of which account should be taken; persons should be sent there, if possible, who by their life and learning may undo the evil opinion founded on false reports (VII.2.D[622]).

In the sixteenth century, and in the mind of Ignatius, the metaphor of the cockle could apply to any place under the influence of the Reformers, or where civic authorities placed obstacles in the way of the proclamation and teaching of the Catholic faith. But Ignatius had in mind especially those places where the Society itself had been defamed or persecuted, and where as a result its credibility was being undermined or had actually been lost. He had gone through such an experience himself in Rome during 1538, and this was not an isolated incident. We notice again the stress on the fruit of the Society's work. In sending Jesuits, 'who by their life and learning may undo the evil opinion founded on false reports', the object is not to avoid any future persecution or humiliation for the Society but to clear the way for the proclamation of the gospel.[39]

---

[38] See chapter 6.

[39] This theme recurs in part X: 'Similarly, when an unfavourable attitude is noticed in some persons, especially in persons of importance, prayer ought to be offered for them and the suitable means should be employed to bring them to friendship, or at least to keep

End Note

Underpinning the process of missioning to the Lord's vineyard, which is the substance of part VII, lies the manifestation or account of conscience. It is this exercise that establishes and nurtures the right relationship between superior (the one who sends) and member (the one who is sent). Their mutual discernment is the fruit of the integrity of that relationship. The member relies on the spiritual sagacity of the superior, and the superior on the transparency of the member. Only with this generous and willing co-operation of the member can the superior fulfil his responsibility of 'sending' in the most apostolically effective manner. An extended exposition of the manifestation of conscience will be given in chapter 6.

---

them from being hostile. This is done, not because contradiction and ill-treatment are feared, but so that God our Lord may be more served and glorified in all things through the benevolence of all these persons.' (X. B [824])

5.

UNION OF THE DISPERSED

CORPORATE MISSION can only emanate from a body that is united. The more such mission involves dispersal to the ends of the earth the more crucial union becomes. Jesuits have to forge and nurture their union and find structures that will support it. Hence the importance of part VIII in the *Constitutions*. Its title indicates precisely its focus and purpose: 'Helps toward uniting the dispersed members with their head and among themselves'. It can be misleading to refer to this part as dealing with 'community'. In contemporary usage the word 'community' spontaneously evokes images, expectations and ideas around *local* community. But the *Constitutions* are speaking about the whole body of the Society. The presumption is that the members are mostly distant from one another, are already dispersed in the vineyard of the Lord. Whether they are alone or in groups, travelling or in a fixed abode, is not the immediate issue. This rather is how to maintain, foster and even increase union in a body whose membership is large, multinational, culturally diverse, engaged in a variety of ministries and physically dispersed. It may be said that part VIII tries to deal with some of the consequences of generously implementing part VII.[1]

The word *comunidad* occurs only four times in the *Constitutions*, and never referring to a local Jesuit community.[2] In fact, these references are primarily to civic communities or associations. Where we would tend of speak of local communities, the *Constitutions* refer more casually to 'the houses where they happen to be' (VI. 3. 3 [585]). This surprisingly imprecise phraseology indicates how much the early Jesuits took for granted the overriding priorities of the mobility and availability required by mission. When a group of Jesuits did live together it was only

---

[1] The fullest discussion of this topic is by Javier Osuna, *Amigos en el Señor: Unidos para la dispersión* (Bilbao: Mensajero, 1997): English translation of part 1 by Nicholas King, as *Friends in the Lord* (London: Way Books, 1974).
[2] IV. 1. D [316], VII. 2. K [628], IX. 1 [719], X. 6 [817].

because, and for as long as, that arrangement was supportive of their mission. Their corporate ideal and self-image were perhaps best expressed in the meaning given to their Fourth Vow of obedience to the Pope:

> The intention of the fourth vow pertaining to the pope was not for a particular place but for having the members dispersed throughout the various parts of the world. For those who first united to form the Society were from different provinces and realms and did not know into which regions they were to go, whether among the faithful or the unbelievers; and therefore, to avoid erring in the path of the Lord, they made the promise or vow in order that His Holiness might distribute them for the greater glory of God, in conformity with their intention to travel throughout the world and, when they could not find the desired spiritual fruit in one place, to pass on to another and another, ever seeking the greater glory of God our Lord and the greater aid of souls. (VII.1.B[605])

The rapid growth in numbers in the early Society also provided a real challenge to union. All this was the context in which the search for union was experienced as problematic and, at the same time, imperative. It should be clear, therefore, that the word 'community', if it is to be used at all in the context of part VIII, needs to take on a much broader and more flexible meaning than is common in our vernacular. In the Preamble it is clear that for Ignatius the fundamental corporate entity, the primary community, is 'the body of the Society as a whole, whose unity, good government, and preservation in well-being for the greater divine glory are primarily in view', that is, in the writing of the *Constitutions* (Preamble 2[135]). This worldwide body is the community that a Jesuit joins and into which he is gradually incorporated. He does not join a particular province, still less a local residence. In recent times this vision has been restated with great clarity:

> Moreover, it is in companionship that the Jesuit fulfils his mission. He belongs to a community of friends in the Lord who, like him, have asked to be received under the standard of Christ the King. This community is the whole body of the Society itself, no matter how widely dispersed over the face of the earth. The particular local community to which he may

belong at any given moment is, for him, simply a concrete—
if here and now a privileged—expression of this worldwide
brotherhood.[3]

This text leaves no doubt as to the priority enjoyed by the
universal body over any particular local manifestation of it. The
phrase 'to which he may belong at any given moment' corresponds
in its apparent vagueness and imprecision to that in the
Constitutions, 'the houses where they happen to be' (VI.3.3[585]).
Yet there is also a recognition that the local community, however
temporary and transient it may be, is here and now a privileged
expression of the universal body—privileged, that is, for its
members. The local community can be seen as a quasi-sacrament
of the universal body, a sign that by its immediacy and tangibility
effectively makes the wider reality present. It can also be
understood as a local incarnation of the universal spirit of the
Society.[4]

Nadal's Vision

Nevertheless, the role of local community, even though important,
is always subordinate to that of the universal community. This
understanding reverses that of the older orders, both monastic
and mendicant (such as the Dominicans). In these the priority is
given to the local community. This difference in the Jesuit model
needs to be emphasized because from time to time in the history
of the Society expectations around local community have surfaced
that do not harmonize with what Ignatius had in mind. His
view, both as regards exterior lifestyle and interior attitudes, is
closer to that of his favoured spokesman and interpreter, Nadal.
In the last chapter we quoted a few of Nadal's most explicit
teachings on Jesuit mission. To these we can add:

> There are missions, which are for the whole world, which is
> our house. Wherever there is need or greater utility for our
> ministries, there is our house.[5]

---

[3] *General Congregation 32*, decree 2, 'Jesuits Today', nn.15–16, in *Jesuit Life and Mission Today*, 293.
[4] Using the imagery of Dominique Bertrand's *Un corps pour l'Ésprit*. I shall add some further reflections on local Jesuit community at the end of this chapter.
[5] MHSJ MN 5, 469–470.

> We have to look up and strive for that great aim of the Society, which consists not so much in living in houses and therefrom helping the city or town or even the neighbouring villages, as in being engaged in pilgrimages undertaken through a mission from the Holy Father or from our own Superiors to help souls anywhere, on any occasion, in any way, whether we be sent to pagans, to Muslims, to heretics or to Christians who perish or who are in danger because they lack shepherds or are neglected by them.[6]

We recall that Nadal had written of Jesuits: '... only let them strive in some small way to imitate Christ Jesus who had nowhere on which to lay his head and who spent all his years of preaching in journey'.[7] He is referring directly to the gospel text that reads:

> As they travelled along they met a man on the road who said to him, 'I will follow you wherever you go'. Jesus answered, 'Foxes have holes and the birds of the air have nests, but the Son of Man has nowhere to lay his head' (Luke 9: 57–58).

These words are often seen as among the 'hard sayings' of Jesus and they certainly have implications of asceticism and self-denial. However, they need to be set in the wider context of Luke's structuring of his Gospel around the theme of 'journey', of Jesus' ministry overall, and most especially of the kind of relationship that Jesus is offering his disciples. These three themes, taken together, evoke that scriptural image so dominant in the imaginations of both Ignatius and Nadal: Jesus and his close companions travelling constantly on the roads of Galilee, moving from town to town and village to village (and ultimately to Jerusalem), proclaiming the Good News of the Kingdom.

Tension between Dispersal and Union

But even Jesus and his close companions were not always physically together as a group. Another governing image for Ignatius, as we

---

[6] Jerónimo Nadal, *Scholia in constitutiones*, edited by Manuel Ruiz Jurado (Granada: Facultad de Teología, 1976), 145. Cited in de Aldama, *Missioning*, 11.
[7] MHSJ MN 5, 773.

have already seen, is that of Jesus sending out his disciples on mission. 'After this the Lord appointed seventy-two others and sent them out ahead of him, in pairs, to all the towns and places he himself was to visit.' (Luke 10:1) *They were dispersed.* The lifestyle that Jesus had first chosen for himself, that of a wandering rabbi, soon became that of his disciples too. So tension between companionship and dispersal is already there on the gospel pages. This tension will become even more acute in the post-Pentecost period when the mission expands from one solely to the House of Israel to being a mission to the entire world.

> You will receive power when the Holy Spirit comes on you, and then you will be my witnesses not only in Jerusalem but throughout Judea and Samaria, and indeed to the ends of the earth (Acts 1:8).

This tension between companionship and dispersal for mission was, in their turn, faced by the early companions in the Deliberation of 1539,[8] and it can be identified as the pervasive issue for part VIII. Before looking more closely at the text, one further scriptural image may help. John wrote of the Word being made flesh and pitching his tent among us (John 1:14). While this metaphor expresses John's belief that Jesus, although divine, became as one of us on earth, we can also say that throughout his public life Jesus continued to pitch tents rather than to build houses. He did not need a house of his own since he was always on the move.[9] This same metaphor of pitching a tent is also helpful in expressing the spirit of the Society and fits well with an Ignatian view of life as journey or pilgrimage.

So what have the *Constitutions* to say in dealing with this tension in Jesuit life? In the first paragraph of part VIII we read:

> For the Society cannot be preserved or governed or, consequently, attain the aim it seeks for the greater glory of

---

[8] See the discussion of the Deliberation of 1539 in chapter 1.

[9] This lifestyle choice can also be linked with Jesus' celibacy. Having nowhere to lay his head indicates not just being constantly on the move, but not having a home in the sense that a married man would have one.

God unless its members are united among themselves and
with their head (VIII. 1. 1 [655]).

Why might this be so? As indicated above, one of the ways in
which Ignatius conceived of the Society was on the model of the
relationship between Jesus and his disciples during the public
life. He hoped that the members would have the same love for
one another that Jesus wanted to be the sign of his love for his
disciples. 'This is my commandment, that you love one another
as I have loved you.' (John 15:12) Much as Ignatius appreciated
and made use of the category of 'order',[10] this was never to be
simply the order of a well-structured and smoothly running
organization, but that which comes from the presence of the
Spirit of love. It is the 'order' that is *communio*.

But besides this overtly evangelical motivation, Ignatius also
realised that union was crucial for other, more pragmatic reasons.
The Society was a new phenomenon in the Church and as such
open to attack from those who believed its innovations contrary to
traditional values in religious life.[11] Disunity among Jesuits would
only provide fuel for such attacks. Furthermore, the Society's
mission brought it into close contact with rulers and leaders who
were often at loggerheads, even at war, with one another and
with the Pope. If Jesuits, for nationalistic or ideological reasons,
began to take sides in these political disputes, the resulting disunity
could destroy the Society. The Society's mission also took its
members into areas of religious and theological controversy where
imputations of heresy were hurled by all sides. If Jesuits were
not strongly bonded with each other in such circumstances, the
resulting disharmony would only make accusations of heresy
more credible. All these concerns, and others that are reflected
in the *Constitutions*, gave Ignatius the motivation to think deeply
about the means that would preserve the dispersed members in
a stable and enduring union.

---

[10] I am not referring here to the canonical term '(religious) order' but to the category of
order (and disorder) that plays so large a part in the Spiritual Exercises. See also the
appearance of the word in VIII. 1. 2 [657].
[11] See the beginning of chapter 2, as well as the references given there.

Divisions in Part VIII

There is a twofold division in part VIII. The first chapter deals with what we have grown accustomed to calling 'union of minds and hearts'.[12] Alternative terms might be 'spiritual union' or *communio*. The remaining chapters, 2 to 7, treat of General Congregations in all their complexity. These are two distinct issues (spiritual union and General Congregations), although clearly related. Different views have been taken on how to understand their relationship. It is a question that I shall not be pursuing here, since I want to focus above all on spiritual union as presented in the first chapter. However, some comments by de Aldama will give a taste of the debate:

> The congregations of the Society have sometimes been viewed as one more means to achieve the union of hearts. But there is no evidence in the *Constitutions* that such was Ignatius' thought. 'The union of persons in congregations or chapters' means the physical gathering of the members of the Society, not 'personal' union in the sense of a spiritual bond. Moreover, Ignatius and his companions looked upon these meetings as something that came in the way of the apostolate and wanted to reduce them as much as possible.[13]

In earlier drafts of the *Constitutions* the present chapter 1 consisted of three chapters. The division of material involved is indicated at the end of VIII. 1. 1 [655]:

> With respect to the union of hearts, some things will be helpful on the side of the subjects, others on the side of the superiors, and others on both sides.

This earlier division remains the structure of chapter 1, with VIII. 1.2 [657] introducing reflections 'on the side of the subjects', VIII. 1.6 [666] introducing matters 'on the side of the superior general', and VIII. 1.8 [671]) dealing with helps 'on both sides'.

---

[12] 'The Union of Minds and Hearts' is the title given to decree 11 of General Congregation 32 (*Jesuit Life and Mission Today*, 339–352).
[13] Antonio M. de Aldama, *The Constitutions of the Society of Jesus: Union among Jesuits*, translated and abridged by Ignacio Echániz (St Louis: Institute of Jesuit Sources, 1998), xiv.

Admissions Policy

Ignatius surprises by beginning with a discussion of admissions policy in the Society.

> On the side of the subjects, it will be helpful not to admit a mob of persons to profession, and to retain only selected persons even to be formed coadjutors or scholastics (VIII. 1.2[657).

How should we translate the Spanish phrase, *mucha turba de personas,* and in particular the word *turba?* One can do so uncontroversially by using the word 'crowd', which is neutral and does not have any negative overtones (Ganss, Divarkar). Or one can give it a pejorative meaning by translating it as 'mob' (Padberg, above) or 'horde' (Echániz). Did Ignatius mean the word to convey such negativity? It is clear that he did, especially in the light of the sentence that follows:

> For a crowd [*multitud*] of persons whose vices are not well mortified is incapable of order and likewise of unity, so necessary in Christ our Lord for preserving the Society's well-being and proper functioning.

This judgment clarifies what he means by a *turba.* We note the way in which Ignatius associates 'order' and 'unity'. The Declaration that follows (VIII. 1.B[658]) makes even clearer that the problem does not lie with large numbers as such, but with large numbers that are made up of unmortified persons (*turba*). These are unfree (not 'indifferent') within themselves, hence prone to disorder and disruptive of union. Moreover, one might add, they are unavailable for mission. Selectivity and discernment in the Society's admissions policy are therefore vital. An abundance of applicants is not to be feared: 'Rather, the injunction is against too easily passing as suitable those persons who are not, especially for admission among the professed' (VIII.1.B[658]). These principles will be spelt out in greater detail in part X (X.7[819]).

This teaching represents a change of attitude in Ignatius that was later recorded by Ribadeneira:

> Although in the beginning he did not make difficulties about admitting people into the Society, he came later to tighten his

hand, and to say that if one thing would cause him to want to live longer ... it would be to make it difficult to enter the Society.[14]

Ignatius had learnt a hard lesson over the years, and especially from events in Portugal. In that Province an uncontrolled admissions policy under Simão Rodrigues had caused incalculable trouble and harm to the Society.[15] Ignatius had also found that some men whom he desired to have in the Society because of their learning did not combine these natural talents with sufficient Christian virtue. He comments on this as he introduces part IV:

> However, those who are both good and learned are relatively few; and even among these few, most are already seeking rest from their labours. We have thus found it a quite difficult matter to increase the numbers of this Society with such good and learned men, in view of the great labours and the great abnegation of self which are required in the Society. (IV.A[308])[16]

Abnegation of self leads not only to inner freedom, but also to genuine humility. Only members who are both mortified and truly humble will be able to live and work in harmony and preserve the union of the body.

Obedience in Service of Union

The discussion of the appropriate admissions policy is followed by one on obedience. 'Since this union is produced in great part by the bond of obedience, this virtue should always be maintained in its vigour' (VIII. 1. 3 [659]). Obedience is a complex virtue with ascetical, mystical, apostolic and unitive dimensions. The high

---

[14] MHSJ FN 3, 611. Also FN 2, 475–476.

[15] Even outside Portugal, the growth of the Society was too rapid and its consolidation was consequently impeded. In 1540 there were 10 Jesuits; in 1556 (the year of Ignatius' death) there were approximately 1,000. After that the pace of growth accelerated even more, until in 1580 there were 5,000 and in 1615 the number had reached 13,000. See Thomas H. Clancy, *An Introduction to Jesuit Life: The Constitutions and History through 435 Years* (St Louis: Institute of Jesuit Sources, 1976), 121.

[16] This realisation led to the decision to admit to the Society not only mature men who were already well educated (usually priests), but boys or young men whom the Society would provide with the necessary education. Hence the origin of the colleges.

point of Jesuit obedience is the generous acceptance of being missioned, of being sent into the Lord's vineyard. However, here in part VIII, this core apostolic thrust of the vow of obedience is taken as a given, and the focus is on its unitive dynamic. The vow not only produces a juridical bond but, when lived in a genuinely religious manner, leads to and expresses the inner union of heart and mind and will. All of this presupposes a deep commitment to the end of the Society *and* a conviction that this end is essentially corporate. Just as the primary community that a Jesuit joins is the universal body of the Society, so too the primary mission is that received by the Society as a body, in which the individual Jesuit then shares.

A serious failure in obedience, therefore, is not just a matter of personal morality — of the observance of a vow — but a wound to the body and a divisive factor in its life. As he had taken a strict line on admissions, Ignatius takes an equally strict one on dismissals.

> Anyone seen to be a cause of division among those who live together, estranging them either among themselves or from their head, ought with great diligence to be separated from that community [*congregación*],[17] as a pestilence which can infect it seriously if a remedy is not quickly applied (VIII. 1. 5 [664]).

What is at issue here is not so much a single act of disobedience as the lack of an obediential attitude expressed through a carping, critical, contumacious, negative, divisive spirit. Such a spirit is contagious; it spreads its influence like that of a pestilence (Ganss, Padberg above) or a cancerous growth (Divarkar). Separation, if deemed necessary, may involve either a transfer to another house or complete dismissal (VIII. 1. F[665]). Ultimately the question is one of the common good. A disunited or fragmented body will be less apostolically effective and the end of the Society will be thwarted.[18]

---

[17] The following Declaration (VIII. 1. F[665]) makes clear that the word *congregación*, and even the phrase 'those who live together', apply both to a local community and to the universal body of the Society.

[18] The reliance on obedience, even its forceful imposition, in order to bring about and maintain unity can be destructive of individuals and of society. For example, the idealization of obedience in Nazi Germany, with slogans such as *ein Reich, ein Volk, ein*

Subsidiarity

Linked to obedience, though not exactly identical with it, is what Ignatius calls 'the properly observed subordination of some superiors to others, and of subjects to superiors' (VIII.1.4[662]). In modern terms, Ignatius invokes and applies the principle of subsidiarity. In his usual manner of imaging reality hierarchically, he sees an upward movement of obedience (VIII.1.4[662]) corresponding to the downward movement of the juridical and spiritual authority of the head (VIII.1.6[666]). Both movements connect members with the head, and the head with the members, through the mediation of persons with delegated authority.[19] But we need to note that for Ignatius subsidiarity is not just an administrative convenience or an effort to improve managerial efficiency. It is much more the outcome of his vision of how the spirit of the Society and the Holy Spirit reside and are active within the body. It has to do with spiritual *discernment* rather than with business organization.

So far the matters treated are 'on the side of the subjects'. It will be evident that this phrase does not mean that these matters pertain *only* to the subjects, but that they involve the subjects in one way or another. However, at this point Ignatius turns more explicitly to what helps union on the side of the superiors, concentrating primarily on the Superior General, who is the focus of union for the whole Society. He begins:

> On the side of the superior general, what will aid toward this union of hearts are the qualities of his person[20] ... with which he will perform his office, which is to be for all the members a head from which the influence required for the end sought by the Society ought to descend to them all (VIII.1.6[666]).

The personal qualities of the General alluded to here will be described much more fully in part IX. But already some aspects

---

Führer, led to dreadful atrocities and the perversion of the common good. Without being firmly rooted in the gospel and in spiritual values, religious obedience too can be perverted, aiming at the wrong kind of union and using immoral means to attain it.

[19] This matter will be treated at greater length in part IX. See chapter 6.

[20] References inserted in the text to the following Declaration (VIII.1.G[667]) and to IX.2.1–2[723–725] in part IX.

of his credibility or moral authority are underlined, especially that of 'his having and showing love and concern for them [his subjects]' (VIII. 1. G[667a]) as well as suggestions for an effective manner of governing (VIII. 1. G[667b]), including the need to be accessible (VIII. 1. 7–H[668–669]). The General is not merely a symbol of the union of the Society but the effective (human) source of that union.

The Chief Bond

We come now to the third division of the chapter where Ignatius addresses the helps to union 'on both sides' (VIII.1.8[671]). Here he reveals the depth of his insight into the theological basis of union. This is one of the richest paragraphs in all of the *Constitutions*, but was inexplicably omitted in the old Summary of the *Constitutions*.[21] It begins: 'On both sides, the chief bond to cement the union of the members among themselves and with their head is the love of God our Lord'. We need to pause on this last phrase. Grammatically the genitive case could be subjective or objective, and this creates a certain ambiguity. In other words the phrase could mean God's love for us or our love for God. However, the whole Ignatian view of reality since his experience at the Cardoner suggests that the stronger emphasis (even if not the exclusive emphasis) must be on the subjective meaning, that is, God our Lord's love for us. Such an interpretation is confirmed by the sentence that immediately follows (see below).[22]

But there is a further ambiguity: to whom does the title 'God our Lord' refer—the Triune God or Jesus Christ? The answer is subtle. In Ignatian usage the title 'God our Lord' denotes the person of Christ while connoting the Triune God. In other words

---

[21] Collections of excerpts from the *Constitutions* existed even before the first text of an official Summary was printed in Rome during the generalate of Laínez (1560). Further additions were made by Mercurian (1590) and his text was slightly revised by Aquaviva. This Summary of the *Constitutions* remained the main source of knowledge of the *Constitutions* for Jesuits until the twentieth century. See *The Constitutions of the Society of Jesus*, translated by George E. Ganss (St Louis: Institute of Jesuit Sources, 1970), 85 n. 29.
[22] We are also reminded of scriptural texts such as: 'And hope does not disappoint us, because God's love has been poured into our hearts through the Holy Spirit who has been given to us' (Romans 5:5); and 'In this is love, not that we loved God but that he loved us and sent his Son to be the expiation for our sins' (1 John 4:10).

it points immediately to the person of Christ, but simultaneously it calls to mind the three persons of the Trinity. In the Latin translation of Polanco the phrase reads *amor Dei ac Domini nostri Iesu Christi*, that is, the love of God and of our Lord Jesus Christ, or (probably closer to his intention) the love of our God and Lord Jesus Christ.[23] This translation suggests that the love involved is both divine and human, that of the Risen Lord Jesus in the bosom of the Trinity. The constitution continues:

> For when the superior and the subjects are closely united to his Divine and Supreme Goodness, they will very easily be united among themselves, through that same love which will descend from the Divine Goodness and spread to all other persons, and particularly to the body of the Society.

The image is similar to that in the fourth point of the Contemplation to Attain Love (Exx 237). There 'all good things and gifts descend from above'. Here in VIII.1.8[671] love is presented as flowing from its source and fountainhead, which is the Trinity. The movement again is *de arriba*, meaning that this love is pure gift from God, totally gratuitous. Notice also that it is *the same love* that unites the members of the Society with God which unites them with one another and, in particular, unites superior and subjects. It is still the love *de arriba*, God's love for us more than (even while not excluding) our love for God. Furthermore, this divine love is not contained within the bounds of the Society but overflows and embraces all God's people. The vision here is broad in scope, mystical in depth, and has fruitful implications for a contemplative approach to mission.[24]

Furthermore, 'the love of God our Lord' will lead to the strengthening of union through charity and 'in general all goodness

[23] MHSJ Const. 3, *Textus latinus*, 223.
[24] This discussion of the phrase 'the love of God our Lord' may be seen as a continuation of the disputes in the sixteenth century between those favouring an ascetical and those favouring a mystical interpretation of the Spiritual Exercises and of Ignatian spirituality in general. Those on the side of an ascetical interpretation will understand the phrase as meaning our love for God; those who opt for a mystical interpretation will propose that it means God's love for us. This ascetical–mystical dispute has never been wholly resolved in the Society of Jesus and continues to surface in different contexts.

and virtues', and also to 'total contempt of temporal things, in regard to which self-love, the chief enemy of this union and universal good, frequently induces disorder'. The insights of the First Week and the Two Standards remain operative. The victory of God's love has certainly been won on Calvary but, subjectively, in our mortal experience, that victory is not yet definitive. It is a case of 'already in part, not yet in fullness'. God's love and its unifying dynamic still clash with the opposing, divisive dynamic of human self-love. Union of minds and hearts requires not only a constant openness to the love of God our Lord, but also an acceptance of the inner purification that follows. Francis Xavier, in one of his letters to Ignatius from Cochin (1549), wrote, 'It seems to me that "Society of Jesus" means to say "a Society of love and conformity of minds"'.[25] All Jesuits may wish to make such a claim for our Institute. However, that description (often quoted as *Societas Iesu, Societas amoris*) will always indicate, not a goal already reached, but an ideal towards which we aspire in humility. We dare not be presumptuous because we are too acutely aware of our frailty in receiving and giving love.

Uniformity or Pluralism?

This constitution, VIII. 1. 8 [671], ends somewhat disappointingly with a statement on uniformity as a value—a topic that does not sit easily with people today.

> Still another great help can be found in uniformity, both interior uniformity of doctrine, judgments, and wills, as far as this is possible, and exterior uniformity in respect to clothing, ceremonies of the Mass, and other such matters, to the extent that the different qualities of persons, places, and the like permit.

It is difficult to understand why this does not form a separate constitution. Uniformity is quite distinct from, and vastly less efficacious in bringing about union than, 'the love of God our

[25] *The Letters and Instructions of Francis Xavier*, translated and introduced by M. Joseph Costelloe (St Louis: Institute of Jesuit Sources, 1992), 217.

Lord'. Ignatius had discussed uniformity at greater length in part III and described the goal that he had in mind in promoting it.

> As far as possible, we should all think alike and speak alike, in conformity with the Apostle's teaching (Philippians 2:2); and differing doctrines ought not to be permitted, either orally in sermons or public lectures, or in books .... Even in judgment about practical matters, diversity, which is commonly the mother of discord and the enemy of union of wills, should be avoided as far as possible. This union and agreement among them all ought to be sought most earnestly, and the opposite ought not to be permitted, so that, united among themselves by the bond of fraternal charity, they may be able better and more efficaciously to apply themselves in the service of God and the aid of their fellowmen. (III.1.18[273])[26]

Ignatius' repetition of the phrase 'as far as possible' in this paragraph, and his customary adaptability ('to the extent that the different qualities of persons, places, and the like permit') in VIII.1.8[671], show that he did not regard uniformity as easily attained. More importantly, he did not regard it as an absolute value, but a relative one. It was a means to an end. But even this nuanced and moderate viewpoint was culturally conditioned and does not harmonize with modern sensibilities. Today's culture puts a positive value on pluralism and seeks for unity in diversity rather than through uniformity.

> More so today than in the past, our membership is drawn from very different social and cultural backgrounds. Moreover, the modern world places a much heavier stress on individual freedom than on the subordination of the individual to the group. Our response to these realities will be to transform them from obstacles to aids in community building. Our basic attitude toward cultural differences will be that they can enrich our union rather than threaten it. Our basic attitude toward personal freedom will be that freedom is fulfilled in the active service of love.[27]

[26] This formulation makes clear the consistent view of Ignatius that union is for the sake of mission.
[27] *General Congregation 32*, decree 11, 'Union of Minds and Hearts', n.16, in *Jesuit Life and Mission Today*, 342.

Internal Communication

Lastly, a body in dispersal requires much internal communication. This need, and ways to meet it, are discussed in VIII.1.9–N [673–676]. Unlike the question of uniformity, Ignatius' policy on this matter sits well with today's cultural consciousness, the insights of social psychology and best managerial practice. Whether this communication is through letters, as was necessary in the sixteenth century, or through newer technological means, the aim remains the same, that is, to promote unity and what the *Constitutions* call 'mutual consolation and edification in our Lord' (VIII.1.9[673]). Without communication, including a flow of information that is accurate and honest, dispersal can first breed isolation, then alienation. In Ignatian terms this is desolation where God is not found.

While this exposition of the need for communication places it in the service of union, it also has a key role to play in governance. A recent monograph by Markus Friedrich[28] discusses this in some depth. Although, for the most part, he leaves aside the dimension of spirituality, the author provides illuminating insights into the thinking of Ignatius and Polanco. He also evaluates the strengths and weaknesses of the system of governance that they promoted. Friedrich writes of 'an unrivalled network of administrative correspondence', and asks what might have influenced the decision to insist on it for the Society of Jesus. He points to three sources or models: the mercantile world (the large firms of the time were international enterprises, like the Society), the Protestant communities (who had a well-developed system of communication to unite their diaspora), and 'early modern political culture in the widest sense' (as in the Italian city-states, and perhaps especially the Papal States).[29]

In dealing with the goal of social unity through regular correspondence (not his main focus) Friedrich says:

> Much more than being simply a fact, unity remained a project for the Society; it was not simply 'there' but had to be constantly

---

[28] Markus Friedrich, 'Governance in the Society of Jesus 1540–1773: Its Methods, Critics, and Legacy Today', *Studies in the Spirituality of Jesuits*, 40/1 (Spring 2009).

[29] See Friedrich, 'Governance in the Society of Jesus', 3–8, for a discussion of these sources.

defended or even created. Letter writing helped to achieve this goal. Especially the communication of edifying news was supposed to incite mutual affection. While the effectiveness of the *litterae annuae* and similar genres in achieving this should probably not be overestimated, they did have an impact. We do know, for instance, that circular letters helped recruit missionaries. We also know that some of the edifying stories were quickly transformed into theatrical performances in order to foster Jesuit identity.[30]

Local Community

From the beginning of this chapter we have stressed that the primary community to which a Jesuit belongs is the universal body of the Society. This mode of belonging is unequivocally essential to Jesuit identity and sets it apart from the self-understanding of most other religious institutes. We also quoted the lucid statement from General Congregation 32 that,

> The particular local community to which he [the individual Jesuit] may belong at any given moment is, for him, simply a concrete—if, here and now, a privileged—expression of this world-wide brotherhood.[31]

This statement relativises the position of the local community while simultaneously affirming its privileged status. It is through the experience of local community that we become progressively more integrated into the universal body. But as a Jesuit may be sent from one local community to another, often many times over a lifetime, his membership of each is always temporary and provisional, while his membership of the body is permanent and unqualified (once he is professed).

The *Constitutions* deal almost exclusively with the universal body. Somewhat as with chastity, although for different reasons, Ignatius does not deem it necessary to include a treatment of local community. Even in his letters there is little that throws light on

---

[30] Friedrich, 'Governance in the Society of Jesus', 16. He also draws our attention (n. 28) to his article, 'Compiling and Circulating the *Litterae Annuae*: Towards a History of the Jesuit System of Communication', *AHSI*, 77 (2008), 3–39.
[31] *General Congregation 32*, decree 2, 'Jesuits Today', n. 16, in *Jesuit Life and Mission Today*, 293.

many of the issues that concern contemporary Jesuits. Admittedly we have the Common Rules, a collection of directives drawn up by him about 1549 to be observed in the professed house in Rome. They soon spread to the whole Society. But rather than offering a stimulating vision of community life, '... they acted to some extent like traffic regulations for larger communities'.[32] His own practice in presiding over that community in Rome (as recorded, for example, in da Câmara's *Memoriale*)[33] does not speak persuasively to Jesuits today. Since Vatican II, official teaching in the Society on local community has been evolving. It combines an understanding of the universal body as adapted to the local situation, with insights gleaned from modern psychology, sociology and theology.

The 35th General Congregation (2008) produced a lapidary statement that challenged many inherited attitudes: 'Jesuit community is not just for mission: it is itself mission'.[34] The first part of this assertion refers to a teaching articulated in General Congregation 32.

> The local Jesuit community is thus an apostolic community, not inward but outward looking, the focus of its concern being the service it is called upon to give men. It is contemplative but not monastic, for it is a *communitas ad dispersionem*. It is a community of men ready to go wherever they are sent.[35]

What the universal body of the Society is in its essence, such also, *mutatis mutandis*, is the local community. *Communitas ad dispersionem*, a community for mission, was and remains an attractive and energizing model for Jesuits. It is readily seen to be in harmony with the mind of Ignatius and the thrust of the *Constitutions*. We are called to mission, as a body and as individuals, and every other value or structure is in service of that call. When we live together, for a short or long period of time, it is always in a *communitas ad dispersionem*. Local community is one of the

---

[32] O'Malley, *The First Jesuits*, 338.

[33] See da Câmara, *Remembering Iñigo*.

[34] *General Congregation 35*, decree 3, 'Challenges to Our Mission Today: Sent to the Frontiers', n. 41, in *Jesuit Life and Mission Today*, 754.

[35] *General Congregation 32*, decree 2, 'Jesuits Today', n. 17, in *Jesuit Life and Mission Today*, 293.

corporate supports of mission. It is only by caricaturing this model that one could accuse it of being inhuman or overly pragmatic, or of denying the value of relationships within the community. As General Congregation 35 said,

> To live this mission in our broken world, we need fraternal and joyful communities in which we nourish and express with great intensity the sole passion that can unify our differences and bring to life our creativity. This passion grows out of our ever new experience of the Lord, whose imagination and love for our world are inexhaustible.[36]

The idea of local Jesuit community as being itself mission is new. It seems to have been first proposed by the Superior General Peter-Hans Kolvenbach,[37] before being taken up by General Congregation 35. It is difficult to see it as in continuity with Ignatius' thought.[38] Indeed, its monastic overtones might have alarmed him. The Congregation did not elaborate on this teaching and so there are many questions left unasked and unanswered. The relevant sentence comes at the end of a paragraph that reads in full:

> Our mission is not limited to our works. Our personal and community relationship with the Lord, our relationship to one another as friends in the Lord, our solidarity with the poor and marginalised, and a lifestyle responsible to creation are all important aspects of our lives as Jesuits. They authenticate what we proclaim and what we do in fulfilling our mission. The privileged place of this collective witness is our life in community. Thus, Jesuit community is not just for mission; it is itself mission.[39]

This contextualising of the final sentence offers no more than a partial explanation of the thinking behind it. We need to turn

---

[36] *General Congregation 35*, decree 2, 'A Fire that Kindles Other Fires: Rediscovering Our Charism', n. 27, in *Jesuit Life and Mission Today*, 743.

[37] Peter-Hans Kolvenbach, letter to the whole Society, 'Sur la vie communautaire', *Acta Romana Societatis Iesu*, 22/3 (1998), 276–289.

[38] This is not intended as a negative judgment on the idea itself. Certain discontinuities may be allowed, or even regarded as necessary, so long as they do not undermine the original charism.

[39] *General Congregation 35*, decree 3, 'Challenges to Our Mission Today: Sent to the Frontiers', n. 41, in *Jesuit Life and Mission Today*, 754.

also to an unease among Jesuits with the rise of individualism in contemporary culture and the consequent breakdown of community in secular society. This includes, but is not confined to, family breakdown. Individualism is also the source of many of the world's inequalities and other injustices. Against this background Jesuit community is then seen as a counter-cultural witness, a lived expression of the possibility of people living together in amity, sharing all that they have and united in a common goal. It is still a community for mission (this must never be lost sight of) but, through the harmony among its members and its openness to others (hospitality comes to the fore—a monastic virtue!), it is itself a mission in today's world.

6.

GOVERNANCE AS PROVIDENCE

AT A TIME WHEN MANY religious orders are adopting (to a greater or lesser extent) models of management taken from the corporate sector, it is good to explore an alternative tradition of governance. As with other dimensions of religious life, Ignatius' teaching on governance is to be found in many different contexts throughout the *Constitutions* and (in applied form) in the letters. However, part IX addresses governance directly and explores many aspects of its function within the body of the Society. The focus is especially on the Superior General and his role as 'the Society's head'.

I want to stress particularly the presuppositions or assumptions that Ignatius had when writing about this topic. In many respects these presuppositions are the most significant aspects of his teaching. However, they can be too easily taken for granted or glossed over as people rush impatiently to the structural and the practical. Jesuit governance is *spiritual* governance, based on certain spiritual experiences, principles and goals. It is quite different from contemporary corporate management. I begin, therefore, by looking at some of these Ignatian presuppositions.[1]

The Society's Head

All authority in the Society of Jesus, whether that of the General, of Provincials, or of other superiors, delegates or directors of works, is a sharing in God's authority. This massive claim is a matter of *faith* and would be a nonsense to an unbeliever. Such faith is presumed to be present and alive in the one exercising authority as well as in the one living under that authority. Some indirect light can be shone on this by examining the phrase 'the Society's head'. The title of part IX is 'The Society's head, and the government which descends from it'. But this use of the word 'head' to refer to the General was a late development. Polanco

---

[1] See Jacques Lewis, *Le gouvernement spirituel selon S. Ignace de Loyola* (Montreal: Desclée de Brouwer, 1961).

recorded that the early companions, before coming to Rome in 1537, had decided to call themselves the 'Company of Jesus' because 'they had no head among themselves, nor any superior except Jesus Christ'.[2] Later, in 1546, in the Deliberation on Poverty, Ignatius wrote,

> When, with complete unanimity, all ten of us chose this poverty, we took as our head Jesus himself, our Creator and Lord, to go forward under his banner, to preach and exhort, as is our profession.[3]

And in the *Spiritual Diary* he recorded,

> Jesus came into my thoughts, and I felt impelled to follow him, for to my mind it seemed that since He was the head of the Society, He was a greater argument for having complete poverty than all other human reasons.[4]

There is no reference in the documentary sources to a human person being referred to as head of the Society until about 1547 or 1548.[5] At this point, however, it becomes apparent that the meaning of the word is not univocal. When applied to Jesus, 'head' designates the King who calls on us to join in his project (Exx 91–98). He is 'our supreme commander and Lord', the 'supreme commander of the good people', 'the Lord of all the world' who in the Two Standards sends out apostles and disciples to spread his sacred doctrine (Exx 136–147). When applied to the General, on the other hand, the word 'head' designates that part of the body which is the source of life and movement for the rest of the body.[6] Here we meet another presupposition—that the Society is a body. This is not the first time we have met this term but we need to ask, 'What does this mean in the context of governance?'

---

[2] MHSJ FN 1, 204.

[3] *Saint Ignatius of Loyola: Personal Writings*, translated by Joseph A. Munitiz and Philip Endean (London: Penguin, 1996), 71.

[4] *Spiritual Diary*, 84. The entry is dated 23 February 1544.

[5] Note that, in spite of the implications of the Fourth Vow, the Pope is never referred to as head of the Society—only Christ and the Superior General.

[6] See X. 8 [820]: 'The well-being or illness of the head has its consequences in the whole body'.

The Body of the Society

Ignatius generally avoids two of the more common ways of referring to a religious institute: as a family or as an order. He probably found the term 'family' problematic—too naturalistic maybe, or too monastic.[7] He also eschews the canonical term 'order', probably not wanting Jesuits to regard juridical structures and obligations as being the heart of their life. The metaphor of a 'body' appeals to him much more. It is organic, and stresses the interrelationships between all the members, without drawing comparisons with ties of blood. These relationships include that between superiors and those they govern. All belong to the one body.

The term first appears in the *Deliberation of the First Fathers* (1539).[8] As the Pope begins to disperse them on a variety of missions the companions are forced to examine the future of their relationships with each other. They realise that the casual 'friends in the Lord' paradigm will no longer suffice. This had served them quite adequately while they were studying together in Paris, or travelling around Europe free to make their own decisions. But it did not fit the new reality of being sent by the Pope to different places. The text expresses their predicament with clarity.

> The first evening we came together, this question was proposed: after we had offered and dedicated ourselves and our lives to Christ Our Lord and to His true and legitimate vicar on earth, so that he might dispose of us and send us wherever he might judge we could be most effective—whether to the Indies, the heretics or among any of the faithful or among non-Christians—*would it be better for us to be so joined and bound together in one body that no physical dispersal, however great, could separate us?* (*Deliberation*, n.3, my emphases)

---

[7] Benedict's choice of the term *abbas* (father) for the head of a monastic community shows that he regarded it as a family. On the other hand there is only one text where Jesuits are told that '… they should warmly love their superiors as fathers in Him' (VI. 1. 2 [551]), and one where the Superior General is described as a person who '… neither allows himself to swerve from what he judges to be more pleasing to God our Lord nor ceases to have proper sympathy for his sons' (IX. 2. 4 [727]).

[8] See chapter 1 for an initial discussion of the *Deliberation*.

Here the term 'body' may not have the richer and more complex meaning it takes on in the *Constitutions*, but its appearance is nonetheless significant. It is used in the Deliberation to indicate a more formal structure than the informality of 'friends in the Lord'. It is worth noticing that the companions are not forced into this decision. They could remain as unincardinated secular priests, yet totally available to the Pope and responsible for carrying out his missions. This could be done on an individual basis and each would negotiate his own bed and board, as it were, according to circumstances. Such a way of life would have adequately fulfilled their offering of themselves to the Pope in the preceding year. But the companions want to honour their communal history and so question whether there is an alternative solution, more in line with the way God has been leading them up to now. The way their decision is described gives an indication of what they mean by becoming a 'body'.

> Finally, we decided affirmatively, namely, that since the most kind and loving Lord had deigned to unite us to one another and to bring us together—weak men and from such different places and cultures—we should not sever God's union and bringing together, but rather every day we should strengthen and more solidly ground it, *forming ourselves into one body*. Everyone should have concern for and comprehension of the others for greater apostolic efficacy, since united strength would have more power and courage in confronting whatever challenging goals were to be sought that if this strength were divided into many parts. (*Deliberation*, n. 3, my emphases)

The second question that the companions address in the *Deliberation* concerns the kind of union that would best serve their purpose. After a much more difficult discernment they decide to take a vow of obedience to one of themselves, thus in practice becoming a religious order. So the foundation stone is laid for a structure of authority, leadership and governance that will be carefully worked out in the *Constitutions*. From the beginning one of the aims of obedience is to preserve union, but that union is expressed in terms of a body wholly dedicated to mission.

No individual is named in the text of the *Deliberation*, so we do not know who proposed which arguments, nor if some

speakers (Ignatius, for example) were more influential than others.[9]
Neither do we know whether it was Ignatius who introduced the
metaphor of the body into the discussions. However, he and the
other Spaniards would have been familiar with (even if they had
not studied) the *Siete Partidas*, the code of law that originated in
thirteenth-century Castile and (with developments) remained in
force until the legislation of Charles V.[10]

> Thus, the image of the body—a living unity composed of head
> and members—is a key metaphor in the Ignatian vocabulary
> of images .... It was also current in the Castilian tradition
> which had formed the notions of authority of Ignatius during
> his youth as a *caballero*. The *Siete Partidas*, taking up the
> ancient image of the king as head of the kingdom of which
> the people are the members, developed the metaphor of the
> state as one body: 'The king, therefore, is the heart, the soul,
> and head of the kingdom; and his subjects, as its members,
> should be united to him'.[11]

This metaphor of the state as a body and the king as its head is
readily transferable to the Society as a body with the Superior
General as its head. Culturally this would have been a smooth
transition for Ignatius.

However, besides this cultural background and his
presuppositions in political philosophy, Ignatius was also familiar
with the way in which Paul made use of the image of the body.
For the mature Ignatius this was probably the stronger and more
explicit influence. His usage of the term in the *Constitutions*
is analogous to that of Paul describing the Church as the body
of Christ. It is worth reflecting on what Paul wrote to the
Corinthians:

> Indeed, the body does not consist of one member but of many.
> If the foot would say, 'Because I am not a hand, I do not

---

[9] Neither is its author named. It seems most likely that the companions as a group
composed the outline of the text, which was then written up by one of them—probably
Codure or Favre.

[10] Essential reading on this topic is Rogelio García-Mateo, 'The Body of the Society'. I
draw on this article in what follows.

[11] Futrell, *Making an Apostolic Community of Love*, 53. He cites *Las Siete Partidas*,
edited by Don José Muro Martínez (Valladolid, 1875), volume 2, 172.

belong to the body', that would not make it any less a part
of the body. And if the ear would say, 'Because I am not an
eye, I do not belong to the body', that would not make it any
less a part of the body. If the whole body were an eye, where
would the hearing be? If the whole body were hearing, where
would the sense of smell be? But as it is, God arranged the
members in the body, each one of them, as he chose. If all
were a single member, where would the body be? As it is, there
are many members, yet one body. (1 Corinthians 12:14–20)

Paul goes on to apply this metaphor of the body to the wide
range of service and ministry that exists within the Church. His
list includes 'forms of leadership'. Leadership needs to exist as a
service within the body that is the Church. Leadership is a charism,
that is, a gift or grace given to a person, not for him- or herself,
but for others. This Pauline thinking enables us to understand
what Ignatius meant by the body of the Society, and the place of
leadership within it.[12]

Formed by the Spiritual Exercises

The unity of the body, for Paul, was rooted in the union of
Christians with Christ through baptism. Ignatius was thinking
of this reality, too, but also of the union that exists in the Society
through all having made the Spiritual Exercises. Hence, both the
one who holds authority and the one who lives under that
authority have had a similar formative experience. If we spell it
out in terms of the graces of the Exercises we can say that both
have learnt experientially what it is to be loved unconditionally
by God. Both have known what it is to be a sinner, but a sinner
graciously forgiven and purified. Both have experienced the
attraction of the person of Christ and the urgency of his call and
of his dream for the world. Both have walked with Christ along
the highways and byways of Galilee, as well as along those of our

[12] There is evidence that Ignatius also thought of the Pope and his leadership of the Church
in a similar way. The faithful constitute a body and the Roman Pontiff exercises supreme
authority over, but also within, that body. This monarchical model of the Church is clear
from Ignatius' letter (1555) to Claudius, negus of Ethiopia, to prepare for the arrival of a
Jesuit Patriarch and twelve other Jesuits on a mission dear to Ignatius' heart. See Ignatius,
Letters, 544–549.

contemporary world. Both have faced and been guided through a serious, life-defining election or choice. Both have known what it is to suffer with Christ in his passion and to rejoice with him in his risen glory. Both have learnt, and continue to learn, to find God in all things.[13]

This presupposition of graces received through the Spiritual Exercises is crucial to Jesuit governance. The superior presumes this experience in the member; the member presumes it in the superior. When a Jesuit meets a superior this shared experience means that not only do they have a common language (which *all* Jesuits share) but that whatever difference their current roles have created is subsumed, as it were, by the graces of the Exercises that they have both received. This becomes real in a special way when, for example, a provincial superior meets a member for the purpose of discerning that member's mission (as at the time of the annual visitation of communities). The provincial has the authority to send, but he is dealing with a person who, having received the graces of the Spiritual Exercises, is also capable of discernment. A wise superior will not send a member on mission relying on his (the superior's) own discernment alone. He will wait until he has entered into dialogue with, and listened to, the prayerful thoughts and suggestions of the member. The final decision and 'sending', while that of the superior, will emerge from their shared or mutual discernment.

The scenario sketched here is a powerful illustration of the difference between spiritual governance and contemporary corporate management. This difference would not be visible to an observer of the process. Best practice in management includes many of the values of spiritual governance, such as respect for the dignity of each person and the ability of management to tap into the creativity of the workers. A manager and worker sitting down to discuss the contribution that the worker can make to an organization will look very similar to a superior meeting with a member of the Society. One needs to look at the underlying presuppositions in each case to see the difference. The two Jesuits

---

[13] Similar reflections on the graces of the Exercises appear in chapter 2 in discussing the six novitiate experiments.

believe that the Spirit is at work in each of them and in their interaction. They are not only asking questions in terms of the best way forward, or the best decision relating to this member, but fundamentally they are also seeking God's will. What has God been telling them in their prayer? Are certain options leading them into consolation or desolation? The more explicitly they ask such questions the more authentic will the process be—that of spiritual governance.

Account of Conscience

This leads us to the next point for reflection, the self-revelation to one's superior known as the manifestation or account of conscience. This exercise was given new life as a result of the turn to the sources, mandated for all religious, after Vatican II. This led Jesuits to realise that, while the account of conscience was dutifully practised, it had become too much of a formality and had lost its vitality. In 2005 the Superior General, Peter-Hans Kolvenbach, sent a letter on the topic to all Major Superiors calling for further renewal.[14] More recently the 35th General Congregation also spoke urgently in affirming this practice. Its treatment appears in the document on obedience in the Society.

> Therefore, obedience in the Society is grounded in the desire to be sent effectively, to serve completely, and to create ever stronger bonds of union among ourselves. These three strands come together in the account of conscience. For this reason, the account of conscience is essential to the practice of obedience in the Society. A Jesuit reveals to his Superior all that is happening in his soul, the graces that he has received and the temptations he has undergone, so that his Superior can more prudently and confidently send him on mission. The account is repeated annually so that the Jesuit and his Superior can evaluate and confirm that mission together.[15]

In fact the account of conscience is even more complex than this fine paragraph implies. Openness to a spiritual father was

---

[14] Peter-Hans Kolvenbach, 'Le compte de conscience', *Acta Romana Societatis Iesu*, 23/3 (2006), 554–561. I intersperse parts of this letter with my own reflections.
[15] *General Congregation 35*, decree 4, 'Obedience in the Life of the Society of Jesus', nn. 23–24, in *Jesuit Life and Mission Today*,.

counselled by writers of antiquity such as Basil, John Climacus and, most of all, Cassian, as a means of gaining help with problems of the spiritual life. But even earlier, as Kolvenbach points out,

> St Anthony the Copt, all alone in the Egyptian desert, already recognised that in order to live and grow in his vocation as a hermit, he needed someone else to whom he could reveal the desires of his heart; someone whose authoritative voice could help him become 'fully mature with the fullness of Christ himself' (Ephesians 4:13). To refuse this self-manifestation to another person and to close oneself up in an individualism that cannot put up with either a guide or a witness is to condemn oneself to wander on barren pathways that no longer lead to God.[16]

This teaching was at the core of what became known as the wisdom of the desert. It fused with a parallel teaching on discernment or *discretio*. Both flourished mainly in monastic circles. During the first Christian millennium the purpose of such self-manifestation was exclusively the spiritual growth of the individual. It offered support, encouragement, challenge and guidance.

Ignatius is following this ancient tradition of openness to another person as he emphasizes the relationship between the one who is giving and the one who is making the Spiritual Exercises.[17] In the Rules for Discernment of the First Week, having given the example of the false lover, he adds in more general terms:

> In a similar manner, when the enemy of human nature turns his wiles and persuasions upon an upright person, he intends and desires them to be received and kept in secrecy. But when the person reveals them to his or her good confessor or some other spiritual person who understands the enemy's deceits and malice, he is grievously disappointed. For he quickly sees that he cannot succeed in the malicious project he began, because his manifest deceptions have been detected. (Exx 326)

[16] Kolvenbach, 'Le compte de conscience', 554.
[17] See 'Annotations or Introductory Explanations', Exx 1–20, and the 'Presupposition', Exx 22.

Similarly in the *Constitutions* Ignatius follows this tradition, especially when dealing with beginners. Here he describes the director of novices as,

> ... a person whom all those who are in probation may love and to whom they may have recourse in their temptations and open themselves with confidence, hoping to receive from him in our Lord counsel and aid in everything. They should be advised, too, that they ought not to keep secret any temptation which they do not tell to him or their confessor or the superior, being happy that their entire soul is completely open to them. Moreover, they will tell him not only their defects but also their penances or mortifications, or their devotions and all their virtues, with a pure desire to be directed if in anything they have gone astray, and without desiring to be guided by their own judgment unless it agrees with the opinion of him whom they have in place of Christ our Lord. (III. 1. 12 [263])

This could be a Desert Father speaking. Ignatius, however, wanted to expand this traditional understanding of self-revelation to another person, rethinking and reworking it in the context of an apostolic order. Could the ancient tradition be put at the service of the body as well as of the individual member without diluting or distorting it? Could it be adapted to aid in missioning and governance without the good of the individual being neglected? Such a complex development would require careful thought and, realising that it would be an innovation in the Christian spiritual tradition, Ignatius did not completely trust his own intuition. That this hesitancy was somewhat uncharacteristic of him shows how concerned he was to respect the tradition. He decided to consult a noted Dominican theologian, Egidio Foscarari, on the matter.[18] After careful consideration, this expert expressed the view that what Ignatius had in mind was well founded in the gospel and could with merit be observed.[19]

---

[18] Egidio Foscarari (1512–1564) was Master of the Sacred Palace and later became Bishop of Modena.
[19] MHSJ Const. 1, 342–346. How this use of the account of conscience could be well founded in the gospel is rather a mystery. The important point is that Foscarari gave Ignatius the go-ahead.

We need now to outline the differences between what Ignatius was proposing and the earlier tradition. They number three, as follows:

- The self-revelation is made to a superior rather than to a spiritual father or director. The *abba* in the desert held merely a charismatic authority, not a juridical one. The individual chose to whom he would reveal himself. In the Society the superior receives the account of conscience *ex officio*.[20]

- It is made at fixed times, not when difficulties or problems arise. This normally means at the time of the provincial's annual visitation, although circumstances sometimes alter this arrangement.[21]

- It is an aid to missioning, to governance, not merely to personal growth, as we shall see in more detail below.

The topic is introduced with a certain gravity in the General Examen:

> After pondering the matter in our Lord, we consider it to be of great and even extraordinary importance in his Divine Majesty that the superiors should have a complete understanding of the subjects, that by means of this knowledge they may be able to direct and govern them better, and while caring for them guide them better into the paths of the Lord (Examen 4.34[91]).

The next paragraph (Examen 4.35[92]) teases out further the reasons for such an account of conscience:

1. 'Likewise, the more thoroughly they are aware of the interior and exterior affairs of their subjects, with so much greater

---

[20] Although Ignatius does not spell it out clearly in the *Constitutions*, the self-revelation to the superior does not replace, but complements, the practice of receiving regular spiritual direction as in the desert tradition.

[21] A contemporary understanding of spiritual direction does not limit meetings with one's director to times of difficulty or distress. In fact regular meetings are encouraged and the focus is on growth in the spiritual life rather than on problem-solving. See Brian O'Leary, 'What is Specific to an Ignatian Model of Spiritual Direction?', *The Way*, 47/1–2 (January and April 2008), 9–28.

diligence, love, and care will they be able to help the subjects and to guard their souls from the various difficulties and dangers which might occur later on.' This is known as *cura personalis* or care for the person. It continues the earlier tradition.

2. 'Later, in conformity with our profession and manner of proceeding, we must always be ready to travel about in various parts of the world …. Therefore, to proceed without error in such missions, or in sending some persons and not others, or some for one task and others for different ones ….' Here the account of conscience is seen as a tool for effective missioning. It is not sufficient for the superior to be aware of the apostolic needs to be met in a particular place, but he also needs knowledge of the suitability of the person being sent to meet these needs. Such suitability embraces the person's health, energy and talents, but also his spiritual profile with its strengths and weaknesses.

3. A further reason is, '… so that thus he [the superior] may direct them better, without placing them beyond the measure of their capacity in dangers or labours greater than they could in our Lord endure with a spirit of love'. This last phrase ('with a spirit of love') translates the Spanish *amorosamente* and the Latin *suaviter*. It might be interpreted as meaning that the superior will not place a Jesuit in situations where he will be unable to find spiritual consolation. All of this is a combination of care for the person and missioning.

4. Finally, so that the superior 'may be better able to organize and arrange what is expedient for the whole body of the Society'. We note the movement from the care of the individual, to the effectiveness of missioning, to the good of the body.[22]

In summary: there are three issues at stake in the account of conscience. These are the personal care of the individual, his

---

[22] This last reason does not precisely add a new purpose, different from the previous ones. It simply indicates that the personal care of each member, and particularly his proper and appropriate missioning, will lead to the whole body's being well ordered and provided for, better able to fulfil its purpose of corporate mission.

appropriate missioning, and the governance and well-being of the body of the Society. None of these issues can be separated from the other two. The account of conscience is not only for the personal care of the individual, not only for appropriate missioning, not only for the well-being of the body, but for all three at one and the same time. In light of these personal, apostolic and corporate purposes, the candidate (the subject of the General Examen) and all Jesuits are asked to give their account of conscience 'with great humility, transparency, and charity' (Examen 4.36[93]). Ignatius assumes that they will want to do this as a means to discovering God's will for them. A further assumption is that in this way they will proceed 'with an increase of grace and spirit' (Examen 4.37[94]). Finally, it is hoped that the account of conscience will bring both the individual Jesuit and the superior into spiritual consolation, the final criterion in all discernment.

It is clear that the word 'conscience', as used in the phrase 'account of conscience', is not confined to the area of morality or of ethical values. As with the daily Examen, 'consciousness' may be a more helpful term than 'conscience'. We open ourselves up totally; the exercise involves a complete self-revelation. Kolvenbach puts it well when he writes:

> The transformation of the opening of one's conscience as a form of spiritual care into a revelation of everything that is going on in us so as to receive our apostolic mission, this implies certain consequences which are contained in the *Constitutions*. In spite of the name *ratio conscientiae*, the manifestation is not restricted to our conscience, but rather encompasses our entire personality. This includes our relationships with God and his plans for us, with ourselves and with all those whom the Lord places on our path, in our communities and our families, in our apostolic responsibilities and in all our contacts.[23]

All this is very different from the customary practice in other religious orders, and still more distinct from, even alien to, business

---

[23] Kolvenbach, 'Le compte de conscience', 555.

practices today. As Kolvenbach says: 'Clearly the account of conscience has nothing in common with an interview in which a manager gives an account of his management to the company director'.[24] Yet in our success-driven culture there is always a danger that the account of conscience may become contaminated by such a model and the spiritual core of the exercise diluted. Time and a relaxed atmosphere are needed so that throughout the meeting both superior and member remain attuned to and seek to listen to the voice of the Holy Spirit. Such cannot happen if there is a sense of rush, of having only a limited time, or if either side sees the encounter in pragmatic rather than contemplative terms. Hearing the members' account of conscience (and the missioning that emerges from it) is the provincial superior's primary responsibility.

Portrait of the General

The second chapter of part IX is based on the eleventh of Polanco's *Industriae*.[25] This readily verifiable source is more reliable than da Câmara's typically romanticised view that Ignatius, in outlining the qualities of the General, was giving us a self-portrait.[26] However, García-Mateo is helpful in pointing us to the representation of the temporal king in Exx 91–94, arguing that,

> Here, Ignatius gives us, 'with only a short or summary development' (Exx 2), everything which his age saw as the ideal of a *Christian prince*.
>
> As the Spanish term *príncipe* quite generally suggests, the prince is at the head of the governmental structure. The concept of princehood—of 'principality'—is developed in the treatises regarding the education of heirs to the crown, a genre

[24] Kolvenbach, 'Le compte de conscience', 559.
[25] The *Industriae* consist of a series of documents drawn up by Polanco in preparation for the writing of the *Constitutions*. See MHSJ, *Polanci complementa*, volume 2 (Madrid, 1916).
[26] Having asserted that Ignatius embodied all the rules of the Spiritual Exercises exactly, and also embodied the teaching of *The Imitation of Christ*, da Câmara adds, 'And I must remember many particular cases from which this general conclusion can be drawn. The same can be said about the *Constitutions*, especially the chapter in which he portrays the General, in which he seems to have painted a portrait of himself' (n. 226, *Remembering Iñigo*, 131). Nadal and Ribadeneira wrote in similar vein.

that was common at the time. A key idea in all of them is that of the supreme political power being in the place of God, as Paul's formula had suggested, 'There is no authority except from God' (Romans 13:1). Thus even temporal authority is located within God's plan. In this conception of civil life, the whole body politic appears intimately related to God, in particular the head. In its exercise of government, the head is to reflect the Good Shepherd, and govern with humility, gentleness, and in poverty.[27]

Ignatius inherited a vision of the body politic that he understood to be rooted in the New Testament, developed and fine-tuned by theologians, and applied in documents such as the *Siete Partidas*. He probably never imagined that there could be other models. Even if there were, they would be lacking from a rational and a Christian standpoint. This vision profoundly affected his approach to governance in the *Constitutions* and to the role and qualities of the Superior General. The General was to have the qualities of a Christian prince!

Qualities of the Superior General

We shall have much to say about the interconnectedness of the divine and the human when we deal with part X.[28] This dynamic polarity underlies the whole of reality for Ignatius and its implications shape the *Constitutions*. In part IX it appears explicitly in the portrait of the General that constitutes chapter 2, 'The Kind of Person the Superior General Ought to Be'.

> The six qualities treated in this chapter are the most important, the rest being reduced to them. For they comprise the general's perfection in relation to God, together with what perfects his heart, understanding, and execution; and also the corporal

[27] García-Mateo, '"The Body of the Society"', 19. In a long footnote (n. 22) the author offers many examples. It reads in part: 'The genre goes back to classical antiquity, and was widespread in medieval Europe. Among the most important are John of Salisbury's (1159), *Policraticus* and Thomas Aquinas' *De regimine principum*. Such works were highly influential in Spain and Portugal. The early titles in the second of the *Siete Partidas* sketch out a conception of the king and the kingdom that, from 1348 onwards, became the basis for the image of the Spanish monarch.' He also mentions, among later writers, Thomas More, Erasmus and Machiavelli.
[28] See chapter 7.

> and external gifts helpful to him. Moreover, the order of
> their listing indicates the importance at which they are rated.
> (IX.2.A[724])

This prioritised list of qualities begins with the General's
relationship with God:

> ... the first is that he should be closely united with God our
> Lord and have familiarity with him in prayer and in all his
> operations, so that from him, the fountain of all good, he may
> so much the better obtain for the whole body of the Society
> a large share of his gifts and graces, as well as great power
> and effectiveness for all the means to be employed for the
> help of souls (IX.2.1[723]).

We have already met two of the premises that lie behind this
paragraph. The first is the fourth point in the Contemplation to
Attain Love, 'how all good things and gifts descend from above
... just as the rays come down from the sun, or the rains from their
source' (Exx 237). Everything is *de arriba*. Also *Constitutions*
VIII.1.8[671], where God's love 'will descend from the Divine
Goodness and spread to all other persons, and particularly
to the body of the Society'.[29] The second premise is Ignatius'
understanding of the Society as a body and of the General as its
head. The consequence that he draws from this is that grace is
mediated through the head and flows into the body of the Society,
especially what nourishes its one end, that is, serving the good
of souls. This mediation is not feasible if the General is not
closely united with God.[30]

On this foundation is built the second required quality, which
is excellence in the practice of all the virtues, with charity getting
special mention, along with a genuine humility 'which will make

---

[29] See chapter 5.

[30] Ignatius is not saying that every grace received by a Jesuit is mediated by the Superior
General. For example, his understanding of how the graces of the Exercises are received
by the individual would give the lie to such an opinion. 'But during these Spiritual
Exercises when a person is seeking God's will, it is more appropriate and far better that
the Creator and Lord himself should communicate himself to the devout soul, embracing it
in love and praise ...' (Exx 15). His assumptions about what happens in a Jesuit's personal
prayer would also contradict this view. The mediated graces that he has in mind here are
more corporate in character, graces for the body and for the mission of the body.

him highly beloved of God our Lord and of human beings'
(IX.2.2[725]). Linked with this is freedom from uncontrolled
passions, or what the *Spiritual Exercises* call 'disordered affections'
(Exx 1, 21). This will ensure that he can form correct judgments,
and be so circumspect in speaking that he becomes 'a mirror and
model' (IX.2.3[726]) for his fellow Jesuits, while also edifying all
outside the Society. In addition, 'he should know how to mingle
the required rectitude and severity with kindness and gentleness'
(IX.2.4[727]). Furthermore,

> Magnanimity and fortitude of soul[31] are likewise highly
> necessary for him, so that he may bear the weaknesses of many,
> initiate great undertakings in the service of God our Lord, and
> persevere in them with the needed constancy (IX.2.5[728]).

Notice that the required qualities are becoming more specific to
the exercise of leadership.

After this discussion of the requisite virtues comes the third
quality, 'that he ought to be endowed with great intelligence
and judgment, so that he is not lacking in this talent in either
speculative or practical matters which may arise' (IX.2.6[729]).
The bar is being set very high. We might wonder at the insertion
of 'speculative ... matters' in the text. Is there an implication that
the General may have to adjudicate on the orthodoxy of doctrine
within the Society? In any case this requirement is immediately
qualified by what follows:

> And although learning is highly necessary for one who will
> have so many learned men in his charge, still more necessary
> is prudence along with experience in spiritual and interior
> matters, so that he may be able to discern the various spirits
> and to give counsel and remedies to so many who will have
> spiritual necessities (IX.2.6[729]).

The ability to discern the spirits is more necessary than
learning. We can link this statement primarily with the general's

---

[31] The expansive attitudes described here as *la magnaminidad y fortaleza de ánimo* are
evocative of the *grande ánimo y liberalidad* recommended to the exercitant in Exx 5. See
Brian O'Leary, 'Magnanimity: An Ignatian Virtue', *Religious Life Review*, 50/267 (March–
April 2011), 107–116.

duty of *cura personalis* but also with the discernment needed for the choice of ministries and decision-making about 'whom to send'. We are implicitly brought back to the first quality required in the General—that he enjoy familiarity with God. In (IX.2.6 [729]) the general is presented as a hands-on person—an intention that became less realistic as numbers in the Society grew and its members lived in ever more far-flung locations.

The fourth quality is recognisably human rather than 'divine' in nature. The text describes it as 'one highly necessary for the execution of business' (IX.2.7[730]). It continues:

> ... that he should be vigilant and solicitous in undertaking enterprises and vigorous in carrying them through to their completion and perfection, rather than careless and remiss about leaving them begun but unfinished.

Here we are closest to a secular model of leadership. Yet we must not isolate this text as though it stood on its own. It needs to be read in conjunction with the more explicitly spiritual and moral requirements that precede it.

As in the Spiritual Exercises, Ignatius takes the human body seriously. The fifth quality deals with 'health, appearance, and age', with an appreciation of the qualities of 'dignity and authority', as well as the need for 'the physical strength demanded by his charge' (IX.2.8[731]). The sixth quality looks to external factors such as the person's 'esteem, good reputation, and whatever else contributes towards authority among those within and without' (IX.2.9[733]).

In conclusion, what are the minimum requirements—those without which no person should be elected to the post of Superior General?

> Finally, he ought to be one of those who are most outstanding in every virtue, most deserving in the Society, and known as such for the longest time. If any of the aforementioned qualities should be wanting, he should at least not lack great probity and love for the Society, nor good judgment accompanied by sound learning. In other matters, the aids which he will have (and which will be treated below [IX.6.1– H(789–808)]) will be able through God's help and favour to supply for much. (IX.2.10[735])

There are two concluding remarks that can be made about the portrait of the General.

First, the *Constitutions* themselves acknowledge that it is idealistic (implied in IX. 2. 10[735], just quoted). But this is not to say that it can be dismissed simply because the ideal is unattainable. Its wisdom supplies highly relevant criteria for the election of the General. The use of these criteria ensures that the person elected, although not a perfect likeness of this portrait, will nevertheless possess all the desired qualities to some degree, and the more important ones to a high degree.

Secondly, the *Constitutions* also presume that what is said of the General applies, *mutatis mutandis*, to others in leadership roles as well. This is why this portrait, and the criteria that constitute it, need to form part of the discernment that precedes all such appointments. Ignatius was convinced of the powerful influence for good or ill of superiors at all levels. 'For in a general way, the subjects will be what these superiors are.' (X. 8 [820])[32]

Providence

A further way of illustrating the interplay that Ignatius recognised between the divine and the human is by reflecting on his use of the term 'providence'. This is a key concept in Ignatius' thinking. In the context of governance the term encapsulates much of the theory and theology behind the sixteenth-century understanding of the role of a Christian prince. The word *providencia* occurs 10 times throughout the *Constitutions*, and the corresponding verb *proveer* 36 times. The presupposition in the Preamble already anticipates this frequency: 'since the gentle arrangement of Divine Providence requires co-operation from his creatures ...' (Preamble 1 [134]). In this specific case co-operation with Providence entails the writing of *Constitutions*. This means that a certain human activity—the writing of *Constitutions*—is needed so that God may provide for the Society.

---

[32] One might even add a third remark, that the portrait offers the ideal image of *any* Jesuit. The General, after all, is 'one of us', with the same experience of being formed by the Exercises and by life in the Society.

More generally, human activity is always meant to be a working with, a co-operation with, God, so that through God's working God may meet the needs of God's people. The link, therefore, between Divine Providence and human activity is more intrinsic than extrinsic. It is not that God first provides and then human activity can begin, or that God's activity and human activity run on parallel tracks. Rather, God's active providence is mediated through rightly ordered and benevolent human activity.

What is presupposed in the Preamble about the writing of *Constitutions* is presupposed in part IX about the act of governing. The Superior General mediates God's providence to the Society. Through him God provides for the Society. Hence, as we have seen, the first quality he needs is to be closely united with God—not for his own personal holiness, but that through him, as head, God may provide for the body and its mission. God provides; the Superior General provides—it is the one providence.

This understanding of providence remains constant when the *Constitutions* deal with lower superiors, since they exercise a delegated authority from the General.[33]

> It is thus from the general as head that all authority of the provincials should flow, from the provincials that of the local superiors, and from the local superiors that of the individual members. And from this same head, or at least by his commission and approval, should likewise come the appointing of missions .... (VIII. 1.6[666])

Hence, with this authority, the rector of a college must 'provide':

> After pondering all the factors, the rector should in everything provide what he thinks to be more pleasing to the Divine and Supreme Goodness and for his greater service and glory (IV. 10. 10[437]).

Then, looking to the attitude of the members, those for whom superiors 'provide':

> We ought to act on the principle that everyone who lives under obedience should let himself be carried and directed

---

[33] See also the discussion of this 'subordination' or subsidiarity in chapter 5.

by Divine Providence through the agency of the superior
(VI. 1. 1 [547]).

This clearly hierarchical way of envisaging providence, and
understanding it as expressed through governance, is only open to
criticism if it is seen as the *only* way in which God's providence
operates in our lives.[34] But it is equally possible to find that same
providence at work through our relationships with others and
in the changing circumstances of our lives.[35] Ignatius speaks of
finding God in all things and he never suggests that the superior
is the only mediator of God's loving care. Nevertheless, the role
of superiors in mediating Divine Providence is an essential
component of his understanding of governance in the Society.[36]

---

[34] There is an obvious parallel between the ways in which Ignatius envisages the mediation
of grace and the mediation of providence. Providence can be seen as one form of grace.
[35] The whole of the Spiritual Exercises is built on this premise.
[36] But who mediates Divine Providence to the Superior General? This is the role of the
body of the Society. The otherwise rigid hierarchical structure of authority in the Society
is balanced by the teaching in part IX, chapter 4: 'The authority or provident care
[*providencia*] which the Society should exercise in regard to the Superior General'. Note
how Ignatius equates authority here with provident care; to wield authority is to 'provide'.

7.

TOWARDS THE FUTURE IN HOPE

EVERY HUMAN VISION will inevitably embrace the future. It is an inherent part of the human genius to want and be able to imagine, project and plan for posterity. The Christian vision, of course, transcends space and time, looking forward to the *eschaton* and to eternal life. But before that, like every other human community, the Church too will have an earthly future. The Society of Jesus, as part of that Church, shares the Christian eschatological hope but also cultivates a vision of its own future in time. This is the essence of the final section of the *Constitutions*, which, quite naturally, looks forward. The title of part X reads: 'How the Whole Body of the Society Is to Be Preserved and Increased in Its Well-Being'.[1] This wording takes up the earlier Preamble to the Declarations that begins:

> The purpose of the *Constitutions* is to aid the body of the Society as a whole and its individual members toward their preservation and increase for the divine glory and the good of the universal Church (Preamble [136]).

To be more precise, in part X the stress is on the *corporate* dimension of that purpose: what the body of the Society needs to keep in mind and to do in order to promote its own preservation and increase. The *individual* dimension of that purpose was expressed in similar language in the title of part III: 'The Preservation and Progress of Those Who Remain in Probation'.[2]

---

[1] Herbert Alphonso has challenged Ganss' use of the word 'well-being' (but Padberg has accepted it). He writes, 'The original Spanish *buen ser* is **not** the same as *bien ser* which, of course, is correctly rendered as "well-being". *Buen ser,* however, means being true to its real self—hence our rendering: "basic self-identity" (or "authenticity").' ('Jesuit Constitutions: Aim and Recapitulation [Part X]', in *Constitutions of the Society of Jesus: Incorporation of a Spirit* [Rome: CIS, 1993], 381 n. 1) He therefore translates the title as 'How the whole body of the Society can be preserved and developed in its basic self-identity (or "authenticity")'. I have chosen to stay with Ganss/Padberg, mainly because the official Latin text translates the disputed phrase as *in suo bono statu*: MHSJ Const. 3, *Textus latinus*, 270.

[2] In the three texts cited there are only minor differences in the words used: *conservación y augmento* (Preamble [136]), *conservar y aprovechar* (title of part III), *conservará y augmentará* (title of part X).

It must be stressed, however, that the purpose of the *Constitutions* is not the same as the purpose of the Society. This latter is expressed quite differently:

> The end of this Society is to devote itself with God's grace not only to the salvation and perfection of the members' own souls, but also with that same grace to labour strenuously in giving aid toward the salvation and perfection of the souls of their neighbours (Examen 1.2[3]).

There may be a certain ambiguity in this paragraph as to whether the Society has one or two ends. The point has been much discussed.[3] The key phrase is 'with that same grace', which indicates, however obliquely, that there is only one end. It is the same grace as brings Jesuits into union with God that enables their striving to bring others into that identical union. In straightforward terms, we do not first pay attention to our own growth in holiness, and then look to facilitating the holiness of others. Rather, we seek the holiness of others and that very seeking brings us to holiness and union with God. This 'one end' view is expressed in passages from Nadal such as: 'Emphatically, therefore, we take measure of our spiritual progress according to the intensity with which we take work for the salvation and perfection of our neighbour'.[4]

The purpose of the Society is mission and those ministries through which that mission is effectively carried out. The purpose of the *Constitutions* is to foster the good of the body and the members so that they may be corporately and individually prepared and available for mission. The focus of the Society is on the world into which the members are sent. The focus of the *Constitutions* is on the body of the Society itself.

These distinctions help us to avoid approaching part X as if the preservation and increase in well-being of the Society were in any

---

[3] See François Courel, 'La fin unique de la Compagnie de Jésus', *AHSI*, 35 (1966), 186–211, and, taking the opposite view, Michael C. McGuckian, 'The One End of the Society of Jesus', *AHSI*, 60 (1991), 91–111.

[4] MHSJ MN 5, 127. A certain dualism, as well as the influence of the spiritualities of earlier religious orders, allowed the two-end interpretation to prevail among Jesuits over subsequent centuries. This development undervalued the uniqueness and novelty of Ignatius' contribution to apostolic spirituality.

sense an ultimate end. In relation to mission the Society remains a means, an *instrumentum coniunctum cum Deo* (an instrument united with God),[5] which this same God may use or not use as God thinks best. Our sole responsibility is to nurture the means and leave the outcome with God.[6]

Résumé

The interpretation of part X provides a different kind of challenge to the rest of the *Constitutions*. It seems to lie somewhat outside the dynamic that dealt first with incorporation, then missioning, and finally the corporate supports to that missioning (union of minds and hearts and spiritual governance). Part X looks more like an appendix or epilogue, which is certainly linked to the preceding constitutions but not essential to their completeness. This ambiguity means that part X has been understood in a number of different ways.

The most straightforward, as well as the most common, is that suggested by George Ganss when he writes:

> Part X sums up all that has preceded it in the *Constitutions* ....
> It presents the finished product or fully constituted Society
> towards which everything treated earlier has been pointing
> .... Here he [Ignatius] sketches the fully organised Society
> and its spirit by brief touches or bold strokes intended to
> recall earlier treatments.[7]

From this point of view one is looking to part X for a résumé or a recapitulation of all that has gone before, a summary presentation of the totality of the Society's life in all its richness. There is, of course, some truth in this, since part X certainly revisits earlier

---

[5] This phrase is taken from X. 2 [813] and will be treated at greater length below.

[6] Thinking in terms of ends and means is typical of Ignatius, as we know from a number of places in the Spiritual Exercises. See especially Principle and Foundation (Exx 23) and Introduction to Making a Choice of a Way of Life (Exx 169). The confusion of ends and means is a constant problem for individuals and organizations. Even in a religious institute, a certain corporate arrogance can lead to an attitude that regards the institute's own flourishing as the purpose of its existence.

[7] *The Constitutions of the Society of Jesus*, translated by Ganss, 331 n. 1. He even uses as a running header the phrase: 'Résumé: the constituted Society and its well-being'.

parts of the *Constitutions*. Some key insights and values contained in those earlier parts are once more presented here.

However, if someone who was unfamiliar with the Society were given only part X to read, he or she would scarcely get a clear idea of the nature, aims and way of proceeding of the Society. Yet this result is what we would expect from a résumé or synopsis of the *Constitutions*. At best such a reader would learn about some important Jesuit values, but not how these values come together in an organic whole. Indeed, the core Jesuit value, that of mission, is not mentioned explicitly at all. There is no 'revisiting' of the crucial material contained in part VII.

Neither is there any internal evidence that Ignatius intended part X to be such a résumé. His intention is accurately stated in the title: 'How the Whole Body of the Society Is to Be Preserved and Increased in Its Well-Being'. This is a focused and precisely delimited aim. Every topic dealt with in part X has this in view. Even material treated elsewhere in the *Constitutions* is now being looked at through the particular lens of 'preservation and increase'.[8]

Furthermore, the notion of a résumé is static whereas we have consistently seen that the *Constitutions* are dynamic, organic and developmental. This internal movement in the *Constitutions* does not end at part IX, with part X added on as an appendix that simply sums up what has gone before. On the contrary, the dynamic of the *Constitutions* includes part X, and would not be complete without it.

This is particularly obvious if we take together the three parts that deal explicitly with the body of the Society as a whole: part VIII on how the members dispersed on mission are to be held together in a union of minds and hearts, part IX on how the body and its members are to be governed for the sake of both union and mission, and now part X on how this same body is to be preserved and increased in its well-being—again in service of that same

---

[8] That is, colleges, poverty, repudiation of ambition, not admitting a mob (*turba*), quality of superiors, union, moderation, seeking goodwill of influential people, discreet use of papal favours, health. These diverse topics are being recalled for a specific purpose, not as a mere recapitulation.

union and mission. These three 'corporate' parts form a unity that is complete only when part X is in place.

Parallel with the *Spiritual Exercises*

A more fruitful approach than that of a résumé is offered through a comparison of the structure of the *Constitutions* with that of the *Spiritual Exercises*. In particular, we might look at how each text begins and ends. From this perspective the Principle and Foundation in the *Exercises* corresponds to the Preamble in the *Constitutions*, and the Contemplation to Attain Love corresponds to part X. In both cases the ending takes up the beginning, but in a different key. The ending reinforces an experience that has been deepened and enriched by a long process of development and growth. In the case of the Exercises the deepening experience is that of the exercitant in his or her relationship with God throughout the Four Weeks. In the case of the *Constitutions* the experience is that of the member in his gradual incorporation into the body of the Society, and that of the body in its internal organic development which culminates in its dispersal on mission.

We know that, in spite of appearances, the Principle and Foundation is a Trinitarian and christological statement.[9] Its dry language and logical structure camouflage as much as they reveal the dynamic meeting between divine freedom and human freedom which is about to take place. It points obscurely to this mystery but does not yet unveil it. The unveiling will be the task of the Four Weeks. Nevertheless, the Foundation already invites the exercitant to the *magis*.[10]

By the time the exercitant comes to the *Contemplatio* the word 'love', which was significantly absent in the Foundation, now bursts onto the scene. The *Suscipe* prayer, to be approached with the attitude of 'one making an offering with deep affection',

[9] 'It is now universally accepted that the God of the Foundation is the Trinitarian God of Christian revelation and that the Foundation is directly ordered to the following of Christ.' (Michael Ivens, *Understanding the Spiritual Exercises* [Leominster: Gracewing and New Malden: Inigo Enterprises, 1998], 26 n. 14)

[10] 'We should desire and choose only what helps us more towards the end for which we are created' (Exx 23).

is an effusion of gratitude, trust and total availability. 'Give me love of yourself along with your grace, for that is enough for me' (Exx 234).

The parallel between the vital movement in the *Spiritual Exercises* and that in the *Constitutions* may not be immediately evident. Yet when Ignatius describes his methodology in the Preamble (2[135]) he is pointing to all that is to come throughout the *Constitutions*—their whole dynamic. This includes the body's 'unity, good government, and preservation in well-being', in other words the subject matter of parts VIII, IX and X.

> Moreover, while the consideration which comes first and has more weight in the order of our intention regards the body of the Society as a whole, whose unity, good government, and preservation in well-being for the greater divine glory are primarily in view, nevertheless, inasmuch as this body is made up of its members, and what occurs first in the order of execution pertains to the individual members, in regard to their admission, progress, and distribution into the vineyard of Christ our Lord, it is from this consideration that we shall begin, with the help which the Eternal Light will deign to communicate to us for his own honour and praise.

Part X is as clearly in the mind of Ignatius as he introduces the Prologue, as is the Contemplation to Attain Love as he presents the Principle and Foundation.

Orientation towards the Future

A further point of comparison is that both the *Contemplatio* and part X are orientated towards the future. Like the *Constitutions*, the Spiritual Exercises are not an end in themselves. They are geared to life, and specifically to the life of relationships and service that lies ahead of the exercitants as they end their period of seclusion (or end the Exercises in Daily Life if they are following Annotation 19). The future beckons, and is indeed already present to the exercitants in the offering of the *Suscipe*. This is why the *Contemplatio* can be seen as a bridge-building exercise between the retreat and re-entry into ordinary life. Strictly speaking, it lies outside the formal structure of the Four Weeks, alerting the exercitants to the need of continuing to find God in all things, even in the so-called secular world which they are re-entering.[11] Hence the encouragement that modern exercitants receive to approach the daily Awareness Examen as an ongoing exposure to the *Contemplatio*, a constant seeking for the graces of that exercise.

In part X of the *Constitutions* the emphasis is on the continuity and growth of the Society and on its future as a body capable of carrying out its evangelical purpose. This calls for unceasing insertion into the world in service of Christ, his Church, and all God's people. The context (we might call it the composition of place) is the world, and the spotlight is on the future. Hence the central and dominant virtue becomes that of HOPE. This is immediately emphasized in the opening paragraph of part X, which echoes very clearly the beginning of the Preamble:

> Although God our Creator and Lord is the one who in his Supreme Wisdom and Goodness must preserve, direct, and carry forward in his divine service this least Society of Jesus, just as he deigned to begin it ... (Preamble 1[134]).

> The Society was not instituted by human means; and it is not through them that it can be preserved and increased, but through the grace of the omnipotent hand of Christ our God and Lord. Therefore in him alone must be placed the hope that he will preserve and carry forward what he deigned to begin for his service and praise and for the aid of souls. (X.1[812])

It is this radical hope for the future which offers the best interpretative key for understanding the role of part X. Hope is the graced human response to the promises of God. It springs from an awareness of providence, the faith conviction that God will provide. This radical hope is the attitude and disposition, the atmosphere and milieu, within which the means proposed for preserving and increasing the Society in its well-being are to be implemented.

---

[11] 'It has a contemplative quality which commends its use when the spiritual development of the four Weeks is complete; its content gathers up the themes of the Exercises in their entirety, and it reaches beyond the Exercises themselves to work its insights and attitudes into the texture of everyday life.' (Ivens, *Understanding the Spiritual Exercises*, 169)

Part X will spell out these means more or less in descending degrees of importance: from ways that unite the Jesuit with God (X.2[813]) to the criteria for choosing sites for houses and colleges—they are to be 'in healthy locations with pure air' (X.C[827]).[12] This final paragraph in the *Constitutions* supplies a disconcertingly down-to-earth ending to one of the world's great spiritual documents. It is a concrete example of how human action, both prayerful and intelligent, will always be required—but it is all God's work. That is the Society's hope as it contemplates the future.

A similar expression of hope appears in the *Deliberation of the First Fathers*.[13] We have seen how, faced with the many differences among themselves due to nationality and culture, as well as to individual personalities and points of view, the companions desired 'to seek the gracious and perfect will of God according to the scope of our vocation'. Their account reads:

> Finally, we decided and determined unanimously to give ourselves to prayers and sacrifices and meditations with greater than usual fervour and, after using all our own resources, to cast all our concerns upon the Lord, hoping in Him who is so good and generous that He denies His good spirit to no one who asks with a humble and single heart. Indeed, He gives with largesse to all men, disappointing no one. Certainly, He would not fail us; but so great is His goodness, He would help us beyond our desires and understanding. (n. 1)[14]

This extraordinary hope that the First Companions had in 1539 as they considered their future is the same hope that grounds part X of the *Constitutions*. This is the hope that Ignatius expects to be alive in every generation of Jesuits. It will be a hope that has utter confidence in the providence of God, not as some abstract principle but grounded in the experience of both body and

---

[12] 'The entire text, then, of Part X spells out a definite hierarchy that is to be maintained in the means to be employed for the preservation and development of the Society'. (Alphonso, *Constitutions of the Society of Jesus*, 388) Various authors present the internal structure of this 'hierarchy' in different ways.

[13] For more on the *Deliberation* see chapter 1 (in the context of the genesis of the *Constitutions*) and chapter 6 (in discussing governance in the *Constitutions*).

[14] Futrell, *Making an Apostolic Community of Love*, 189.

members, of being held in the loving hands of God. The Society is safe with God; God will guarantee its continued existence and fruitfulness. What part X invites us into, as the *Constitutions* come to their end, is a *Contemplatio ad spem*, a Contemplation to Attain Hope.

The Divine and the Human: The Cardoner Experience

Central to the wisdom granted to Ignatius was an understanding of the interplay of the divine and the human in life.[15] This can be traced to his mystical experiences at Manresa, and especially to what happened on the banks of the Cardoner.[16] But his treatment of the content of these experiences in the pages of the *Autobiography* is extremely sparse. He refers to what he experienced at Manresa, first naming five experiences: a vision of the Trinity, a new understanding of creation, an enlightenment on the Eucharist, a vision of the humanity of Christ, and a vision of Our Lady. However, it is not easy to be precise about what he actually 'saw'. While he uses several images, there is little detail and not much affective tone. This cannot be simply attributed to a want of an imaginative or affective capability, since there is plenty of evidence that he had both these gifts. But it could be attributed to the lack of a literary proficiency that would have allowed him to communicate such imaginative and affective experiences in words (a quite different matter).[17]

However, there is a further reason that might explain this dearth of imaginative or affective tone in the narrative. It is that the core experience in each vision was not imaginative or affective, but intellectual. This is a crucial point to grasp. We need to notice the phrases he uses: 'his understanding was raised on high', 'it was granted him to understand', 'he clearly saw with his

---

[15] I have referred to this interplay of the divine and the human a number of times throughout this book. It lies at the heart of Ignatian spirituality. Here I offer a longer excursus on the topic.

[16] See the masterly article by Leonardo R. Silos, 'Cardoner in the Life of Saint Ignatius of Loyola', *AHSI*, 33 (1964), 3–43. Also Brian O'Leary, 'The Mysticism of Ignatius Loyola', *Review of Ignatian Spirituality (CIS)*, 116 (2007), 77–97; Gill K. Goulding, 'The Cardoner Imperative', *The Way*, 47/1–2 (January and April 2008), 243–259.

[17] An obvious contrast would be Teresa of Avila who could do both with great facility.

understanding'. These insights impinged on Ignatius, could even be said to have changed his life, but they did not lend themselves to being communicated imaginatively.

When he comes to the 'great enlightenment' itself, which he received on the banks of the Cardoner, there is even less imaginative or affective colour, and an even more direct focus on the understanding:

> As he sat there the eyes of his understanding were opened and though he saw no vision he understood and perceived many things, numerous spiritual things as well as matters touching on faith and learning, and this was with an elucidation so bright that all these things seemed new to him (*Autobiography*, n. 30).

It may even be that Ignatius' primary purpose at this point in his narrative was not so much to convey *what* he had been taught as simply to assert *that* he had been taught. In a more explicit way he had earlier made the claim: 'During this period God was dealing with him in the same way a schoolteacher deals with a child while instructing him' (*Autobiography*, n. 27).

In both cases it is the fact that he was being taught by God which is most important for him to affirm. This is perhaps the first example of Ignatius' tendency to be very concerned to establish his personal credibility (and later, the credibility of the Society).[18] By strongly asserting in the *Autobiography* that God had taught and enlightened him, he is offering his Jesuit readers a legitimisation and authentication of his subsequent decisions, especially those that led to the foundation of the Society.

The passage on the Cardoner experience continues:

> He cannot expound in detail what he then understood, for they were many things, but he can state that he received such a

---

[18] A dramatic example is recorded in the *Autobiography*, n. 98 when Ignatius faced head-on the slanders put about in Rome in 1538 by Francisco de Mudarra and his friends. They were insinuating that Ignatius and his companions were disguised Lutherans and that they 'were fugitives from Spain, from Paris, and from Venice'. Not satisfied with the accusers' full retraction of their calumnies, Ignatius persisted until a formal juridical sentence was pronounced in his and the companions' favour. There were other such incidents both before and after 1538.

lucidity in understanding that during the course of his entire life—now having passed his sixty-second year—if he were to gather all the helps he received from God and everything he knew, and add them together, he does not think they would add up to all that he received on that one occasion (n. 30).

This bold statement does not mean that Ignatius' later mystical experiences, for instance at La Storta or during his years in Rome, were not more profound in terms of intimacy with Christ and the Trinity, but it does suggest that what happened at the Cardoner remained unequalled from a didactic perspective. It was the apex of the process of God's teaching him.

Nadal, too, emphasizes the centrality of insight and understanding when he writes about Cardoner:

> The eyes of his understanding were opened by such a fullness and wealth of interior light that in that light he understood and contemplated the mysteries of faith and spiritual things and truths pertaining to natural enquiry [*quaeque ad scientias pertinent*]. The reality of all things seemed to be manifest to him and a wholly enlightened understanding .... Whenever questions were put to him on matters of importance or when something was to be determined regarding the character of the Society's Institute, he would refer to that grace and light, as though he had there seen the guiding principles and causes of all things.[19]

An embroidered myth gradually grew up around the Cardoner experience. This suggested that Ignatius saw then in every detail the future Institute of the Society of Jesus. Nadal, however, could not possibly have held this view since he was conversant with Ignatius' methodology and struggles in writing the *Constitutions*.

A more balanced interpretation of Nadal's text suggests that what Ignatius learnt at the Cardoner was a deepened understanding of and aptitude for discernment. In this way Cardoner became the touchstone for all his later decision-making. Before that he had begun to notice and wonder (as at Loyola), but he did not understand. He was still, as he says in the *Autobiography*,

[19] MHSJ FN 2, 239–240.

blind.[20] But henceforth there is in him an assurance that was not there before.

This interpretation, of course, gives us little of a concrete nature to hang on to. We naturally seek to discover a more positive content. This partly explains a tendency to interpret Ignatius' description of what happened at the Cardoner as indicating that he was given new knowledge, that the content of his knowledge both of God and of the world was increased. While the text does not exclude such a reading, neither does it demand it. Let us recall again his exact words:

> ... he understood and perceived many things, numerous spiritual things as well as matters touching on faith and learning, and this was with an elucidation so bright that all these things seemed new to him (*Autobiography*, n. 30).

This can readily mean that he was given a new and deeper intellectual grasp of realities, secular as well as spiritual, that he, at least in some inchoate way, already knew. This, I suggest, is the more probable meaning. If he had been receiving new knowledge (in the sense of completely new content) there would be no point in saying that 'all these things seemed new to him', because they would, in fact, have been new to him. But Ignatius was seeing familiar realities in a new light and with a greater sagacity. Furthermore, since he speaks of his Cardoner experience immediately after his description of the five visions at Manresa, it is likely that what he had primarily (though not exclusively) in mind was a deeper understanding of the Trinity, creation, the Eucharist, the humanity of Christ, and Our Lady. These were not new facts, or new truths (new content, as it were), but they seemed as new to him in the vivid intuitive comprehension with which he was now gifted.

Interconnectedness of Truths

Either interpretation (that there was new content, or that there was no new content) allows for the inference that an important part

---

[20] 'Something happened as he was on his way [to Montserrat] and it will be good to record it so that others may understand how our Lord dealt with that soul, still blind but filled with ardent desires to follow Him in every way he knew' (*Autobiography*, n.14).

of the experience was an understanding of the interconnectedness of the truths whose meaning he saw, bringing together matters of the spirit, of faith and of secular learning. This interconnectedness might well correspond to Nadal's phrase about Ignatius' seeing at the Cardoner 'the guiding principles and causes of all things'. Ignatius saw how all things had their source and origin in the creator God. Their guiding principles and causes could be found in the Logos and the Sophia, the Word and the Wisdom of God. They had an order, a meaning, and an orientation given them by God. All of this is implied by the word 'interconnectedness'. Such a reading of the text helps us to understand how the Cardoner experience communicated to Ignatius the gift of discernment. Hence Cardoner could become the touchstone for all his future discernment and decision-making.

Our own difficulties with decisions often have their source in a want of awareness of the relationships, interconnections and interdependencies, not only between the human and secular realities themselves with which we are dealing, but between these and the divine realities which are communicated in the darkness of faith. We need the gift of analysis which dissects the complexities of situations and matters for decision, and that of synthesis that restores unity (but at a deeper level) and leads us to make good decisions.

The understanding of this interconnectedness also allows Ignatius to develop a spirituality which may broadly be called humanistic. I say broadly because the words 'humanism' and 'humanistic' are problematic when applied to Ignatius. He was certainly not a humanist in the modern sense in which the term has been hijacked by atheistic secular humanism. But neither was he a humanist even in the Renaissance and sixteenth-century meaning of the term, in which the New Learning, while not denying the existence of God, tended to put the human person at the centre of the universe. For Ignatius, God was always at the centre and the human person could never usurp that position.[21]

---

[21] 'Ignatius's mystical vision articulated in the language of the modern age turns the modern primacy of the subject on its head and results in a more radically God-centred view of reality than the natural theology of the Scholastics or even the spiritual theology of Gerson and his followers. Rather than starting from the creature and working his way up

So I use the word 'humanism' of Ignatius simply to indicate his reverence for the whole of creation, his valuing of the human person with all his or her gifts, talents and creativity, his conviction that there is a need to foster the human as well as being open to the divine.[22]

It was this sense of interconnectedness, rooted in the Cardoner experience, that gave Ignatius a great freedom in the face of secular learning, neither demonizing it nor canonizing it, but seeing it in its relationship with revealed truth, recognising in both different aspects of the one Truth. And it was this same sense of interconnectedness which allowed the apostolate of education to emerge within the early Society, even though the adoption of this apostolate was in discontinuity with the ideal of mobility in Ignatius' original vision.[23]

Towards Union with God

This excursus on how Ignatius, through his mystical experience at the Cardoner, came to understand the way in which the divine and the human are interconnected, can serve as introduction to X.1–3[812–814]. These are the most profound paragraphs in part X, and among the most profound in the whole of the *Constitutions*. Here Ignatius expresses his conviction of the need

---

to a Creator conceived in accordance with anthropological and cosmological principles, Ignatius posits God as the foundation of all anthropology.' (Louis Dupré, 'Ignatian Humanism and Its Mystical Origins', *Communio*, 18 [1991], 164–182, here 173)

[22] A fairly recent discussion is that of Ronald Modras, *Ignatian Humanism: A Dynamic Spirituality for the 21st Century* (Chicago: Loyola, 2004), especially chapters 1 and 2, 'Ignatian Spirituality' and 'The Renaissance Origins of Ignatian Humanism'. Also John W. O'Malley, 'Renaissance Humanism and the Religious Culture of the First Jesuits', *Heythrop Journal*, 31 (1990), 471–487.

[23] See O'Malley, *The First Jesuits*, chapter 6, 'The Schools', 200: 'We know a great deal about the origins of Jesuit commitment to formal schooling and the context in which it took place. Not all questions have been answered, but the essential framework is clear. What is still surprising, however, is how easily the first Jesuits glided into a decision of this magnitude and how little account they seem to have taken of its manifold impact upon them. The sources never fully satisfy on this issue ...'. Further on he names one of the main unforeseen results: 'The tension between the continuing insistence on the necessity of mobility and the long-term commitment required by the schools would remain throughout Jesuit history' (239). There is no doubt that the Society became less mobile because of its involvement in education, as well as for other reasons. Some of this mobility has been regained in recent years.

for the polarities of the divine and the human to be recognised and then held in creative tension. He shows brilliantly how this can be achieved.

The first of these paragraphs lays a sound foundation for what follows by stressing the divine polarity in the strongest terms:

> The Society was not instituted by human means; and it is not through them that it can be preserved and increased, but through the grace of the omnipotent hand of Christ our God and Lord. Therefore in him alone must be placed the hope that he will preserve and carry forward what he deigned to begin for his service and praise and for the aid of souls. (X. 1 [812])

Human means are acknowledged but their effectiveness is relative to that of God's activity and dependent on it. God alone began the enterprise that is the Society of Jesus. God alone makes its future viable. 'Unless the Lord builds the house, those who build it labour in vain.' (Psalms 127:1) Therefore it follows that,

> In conformity with this hope [in God alone], the first and most appropriate means will be the prayers and Masses which ought to be offered for this holy intention [the Society's preservation and growth].

Intercessory prayer, whether personal, communal or liturgical, best expresses the total reliance of the Society on the initiative of God.[24] Ignatius presumes this constant practice among Jesuits as he goes on to spell out in more detail his understanding of how the polarities of the divine and the human work in collaboration (X. 2–3 [813–814]). These two paragraphs form a unit and are best reflected on together.

He begins the first of these paragraphs by outlining three objectives:

- the preservation and growth of the body of the Society;
- the preservation and growth of the spirit of the Society;
- the aiding of souls to reach their ultimate and supernatural end.

---

[24] Ignatius' custom of seeing the Mass as a powerful prayer of intercession is illustrated in many of his writings and in what we know of his practice.

Then he names four means to attain these objectives:

- goodness and virtue, and especially charity;

- a pure intention of the divine service;

- familiarity with God our Lord in spiritual exercises of devotion;

- sincere zeal for souls for the sake of God's glory.

These are 'the means which unite the human instrument with God and so dispose it that it may be wielded well by his divine hand'. We ought to pay particular attention to this central image or metaphor—that of the human instrument.[25] It emphasizes the primacy of God's action in the world, and the instrumental nature of our co-operation in that action. The third point of the *Contemplatio* reads:

> I will consider how God labours and works for me in all the creatures on the face of the earth, that is, he acts in the manner of one who is labouring (Exx 236).

God is the divine energy, powerful, active and creative. God is working, not just 'for me in all the creatures' (animate and inanimate) but for all creatures in and through me—just as God worked in and through the humanity of Jesus, the crown of creation. Jesus' humanity and ours thus become instrumental in the hands of God for God's redemptive purpose. This applies both to the personal humanity of each Jesuit and to the corporate humanity of the body of the Society.

This is not the first time that the metaphor of the human instrument appears in the *Constitutions*. It is already used in the General Examen in a passage dealing with impediments to admission:

> For, in addition to other reasons, it appears to us in our Lord that, because of the ordinary and common weakness of many persons, those who hope to enter the Society in order to be good and faithful sowers in the Lord's field and to preach his

---

[25] See Dominic Maruca, *Instruments in the Hand of God: A Study in the Spirituality of St Ignatius Loyola* (Rome: PUG, 1963).

> divine word will be instruments the more apt for this purpose, the less they are marked by the first and second defects (Examen 2.6[30]).

Instrumentality is here associated with the sowing and preaching of the word in the Society. God works through the sower and the preacher, but the sower and preacher must be 'apt for this purpose', fitting instruments, and so needing to be free from certain named defects.

In a more generic way, and one that underlines the fragility of the instrument, the image reappears in part VII. The text is urging Jesuits to pray for the Church and for those within it who are of greater importance for the common good; for friends and benefactors, living and dead,

> And likewise for those for whose particular benefit they and the other members of the Society are working in diverse places among believers or unbelievers, that God may dispose them all to receive his grace through the weak instruments of this least Society (VII.4.3[638]).

We might also link this metaphor with the theme of providence that we reflected on in chapter 6. The human instrument mediates God's providence towards God's people; he or she becomes the channel of that providence. God's saving and sanctifying action reaches and impinges on God's people through the instrumentality of those who are sent—the Society and its members.

Communicating with Others

We can now turn to what Ignatius calls 'the natural means which equip the human instrument of God our Lord to deal with his fellow human beings' and which he insists 'will all help toward the preservation and growth of this whole body' (X.3[814]). An instrument has to fit the hand of its user, the artist or artisan, but it also has to be suitable for dealing with the material on which the artist or artisan wishes to work. The most delicate brush, although it feels just right in the hand, will be of little use to a sculptor in marble.[26] Instrumentality is like the Roman god

---

[26] Example taken from Joseph F. Conwell, unpublished notes.

Janus. It faces in two directions—towards the person who makes use of the instrument, and towards the material on which that instrument will work.

Applying this metaphor to the purpose and mission of the Society, which is 'to help souls', we recognise that not only the instruments, but also the material on which they work, are not inert, lifeless substances but living, autonomous human beings. So we are speaking of 'instruments' who freely agree to be such in God's hands, and of 'material' that has the freedom to allow or to reject the work and influence of the instrument. In this scenario, facing in two directions, we as instruments require to be in union with God so that God can work through us, but we also need to know how to relate easily and effectively with people. Ignatius, therefore, in X. 3 [814] selects three so-called 'human or acquired means' for special mention:

- well-grounded and solid learning;
- a method of proposing it to the people by means of sermons and lectures;
- the art of dealing and conversing with others.

In more contemporary language we might speak of the need to be well educated in accordance with the culture and the academic and professional standards of our time. Such education is to be accompanied by an ability to communicate its fruits effectively to others.[27] Even more foundational, and essential to all our ministries, is the need for an agreeable facility in human relationships.[28] The right use of these means then becomes a co-operation with God's work in the world, a sharing in divine providence.

However, the man who composed the Principle and Foundation, the Two Standards, and the Rules for the Discernment of Spirits, was well aware of human obtuseness and ambivalence. He knew how we can be seduced and trapped into unfreedom by the very goodness of creation. Human or natural means easily

---

[27] This links with the stress on rhetoric in sixteenth-century Jesuit educational theory.
[28] See Thomas H. Clancy, *The Conversational Word of God: A Commentary on the Doctrine of St Ignatius of Loyola Concerning Spiritual Conversation* (St Louis: Institute of Jesuit Sources, 1978).

become ends in themselves, or means to ends other than God. So Ignatius lays down conditions for the right use of these natural or acquired means:

- They are to be based upon the foundation of the spiritual means that unite the human instrument with God, not acquired or exercised independently of them.

- They are to be acquired and exercised for the divine service alone, not for our own, or the Society's satisfaction, reputation or glory.

- We are not to put our confidence or reliance on them, but through them co-operate with the divine grace according to the arrangement of the sovereign providence of God our Lord.

The spiritual or supernatural means to preserve and increase the whole body of the Society in its well-being, and the human or natural means that are also necessary, while distinct, are not separate. For Ignatius the unifying element is the glory of God:

> For he desires to be glorified both through the natural means, which he gives as Creator, and through the supernatural means, which he gives as the Author of grace (X.3[814]).

Our personal relationship with God, nurtured by the means outlined in X.2[813], is itself apostolic.[29] We seek God in the awareness of being an instrument, and conscious that this instrument will be purified, enlightened and brought into union with God *through being used.*[30] A corollary to this is that the natural means outlined in X.3[814] are themselves closely integrated with the Jesuit's growth into union with God, as well as being necessary for effective proclamation of the Word. These natural or human means can be seen as sacraments of our hope, exterior

---

[29] We recall that it is 'with that same grace' that we devote ourselves to our own salvation and perfection and to the salvation and perfection of others (Examen 1.2[3]).
[30] Growth through the pattern of the Three Ways (of purification, enlightenment and union) is usually presented in the Christian tradition as taking place in the context of formal prayer. In Jesuit life such growth occurs as much, if not more, in the context of the apostolate. It is here that the Jesuit, the instrument, is used by God. This itself is a purifying, enlightening, and eventually unitive experience.

signs pointing to and making present our total confidence in God's providence in our regard, both individually and corporately.

The three opening paragraphs of part X constitute a text of immense significance—a foundational text for Jesuit apostolic spirituality. They expound briefly but incisively Ignatius' way of bringing together the great polarities of the divine and the human. These polarities are presented, not in opposition to each other, not even simply in interaction with each other, but in terms of compenetration. Such compenetration means that nothing is either wholly sacred or wholly secular. The divine compenetrates the human and the human the divine. Duality is transcended, and all of creation is shot through with grace, Christified.

This is the great integrating vision of Ignatius, rooted in the experience at the Cardoner, which grasps the divine order of the universe and its sacramental character. Sharing this vision the whole body of the Society and each individual member can live lives infused with *discreta caritas*, empowered and missioned by Christ, and confident that God will lead them forward as 'friends in the Lord' into God's future.[31]

---

[31] The theological insights contained in the opening paragraphs of part X underpin all of Ignatius' legislation and praxis in regard to formation. For example, part III ('The Preservation and Progress of Those Who Remain in Probation') and part IV ('The Learning and Other Means of Helping Their Neighbour That Are to Be Imparted to Those Who Are Retained in the Society'). See Brian O'Leary, 'Labourers in Christ's Vineyard: Apostolic Formation in the Thinking and Praxis of Ignatius of Loyola', *Religious Life Review*, 49 (May–June 2010), 143–158, where I present much of the above material and develop the link with formation further. 'What does Ignatius envisage that formation is for? In the sixteenth-century context it was for something quite new in the Church: life in a de-cloistered religious order whose sole purpose was mission. It is important to emphasise that formation was for a *life*, not for some specific part or aspect of that life. This unity (life) is what creates the demand that formation be integrated. Formation must assist and nourish personal growth on the human as well as on the more specifically spiritual levels. It must enable a person to relate and work closely with other "friends in the Lord" (a way in which Ignatius referred to the early companions). And it must *at one and the same time* fashion men who are at home with all kinds of people and who are professionally trained to meet the demands of the ministries to which they are assigned.' (150–151.)

INDEX

abnegation, 39, 50, 52–53, 111
account of conscience, 102, 130–131, 133–136
adversaries, 65; *see also* enemy
affections, 79, 139
affectivity, 53, 77, 79–80, 152–153
Aldama, Antonio de, 19, 98, 100 n. 36, 109
angels, 57, 60–62
Anthony the Copt, St, 131
apostles, 39, 65, 68 n. 18, 82–86, 124
apostolate, 7, 37, 109, 157, 162 n. 29
apostolic, 7–10, 12, 15–17, 26, 31, 36–37, 41, 44, 49–51, 55, 57, 62–66, 74, 82 n. 4, 83, 85–87,
    91, 94–95, 97, 99, 102, 111–112, 120, 126, 132, 134–135, 145 n. 4, 162–163
ascetical, 2, 7, 39, 48, 50, 62–64, 66, 93 n. 25, 111, 115 n. 24
asceticism, 7, 48, 64, 69, 82, 106
attachments, 72
austerities, 8, 63, 73
authority, 18, 62, 91, 92 n. 23, 95, 100–101, 113–114, 123, 126–129, 133, 137, 140–143
Autobiography, 1–2, 5–8, 11–12, 20, 45, 60, 64, 69, 75, 82, 86–87, 152–155
availability, 14, 38 n. 27, 60, 62, 89–90, 103, 110, 126, 145, 148
avarice, 65

Balthasar, Hans Urs von, 25–26, 87 n. 15
Basil, St, 131
begging, 48; *see also* mendicancy
Benedict, St, 28 n. 11, 41, 125 n. 7
Bobadilla, Nicolás de, x, 6 n. 20, 23 n. 56
body (of the Society), 16, 21–22, 26, 41, 55–56, 62, 65, 71, 88–89, 93, 103–105, 112, 115,
    118, 119–120, 123, 125–128, 132, 134–135, 138, 142, 144–145, 147–150, 152, 158–159,
    162–163; *see also* corporate
body (of Christ), 127–128
body (physical), 22–23, 57, 59, 69, 74, 140
Borgia, Francis, 35 n. 23, 75
Brandão, Antonio, 76–78
brothers, 94 n. 26

Câmara, Luis Gonçalves da, 1 n. 1, 2, 4, 5, 20, 100, 120, 136
candidates, 26, 28–29, 31 n. 15, 32–33, 35–37, 39–41, 46, 48–49, 51, 135
Canon Law, 25 n. 3, 31 n. 17, 57–58
Cardoner, 8, 20, 86, 114, 152–157, 163
care of souls, 46 n. 35, 98
Cassador, Jaime, 64 n. 16, 85 n. 13
Cassian, John, 28 n. 11
celibacy, 17, 61, 107 n. 9
charism, 22–23, 52, 73, 121 n. 38, 128
charity, 21, 47, 49, 73, 78, 94, 115, 117, 135, 138, 159
Charles V, 127
chastity, 17 n. 39, 26 n. 6, 38 n. 27, 55–62, 119
chivalry, 3, 7
Christ, 8, 10, 12–13, 34, 39–41, 44–45, 47, 49, 52, 54–55, 62, 64–68, 82–85, 87–88, 96–98,
    104, 106, 114–115, 124–125, 127–129, 131, 150, 152, 154–155, 158, 163; *see also* Jesus
Church, 13, 23, 25–26, 31 n. 17, 35 n. 25, 36 n. 24, 37, 51, 59, 84–85, 91, 98, 108, 127–128,
    144, 150, 160, 163 n. 31

Clairvaux, Bernard of, 69
Climacus, John, 131
Cluny, William of, 69
coadjutors, 27, 34 n. 22, 53, 55, 73, 110
colleges, 29, 56, 68, 78, 84, 93, 99, 111 n. 16, 142, 147 n. 8, 151
commitment, 16–17, 27, 35, 37, 55–57, 59, 66, 79–80, 82, 84, 112, 157 n. 23
community (local), 14 n. 35, 49, 92, 103–105, 112 n. 17, 119–121
community (universal), 36, 41, 58, 87, 96, 103–105, 112, 117, 119–122
companions, ix–x, 3, 5–6, 10–21, 24 n. 1, 34, 36–38, 42, 46–47, 55, 58, 61, 64–65, 82, 87,
     89–90, 93, 98 n. 32, 104, 106–107, 109, 124–126, 127 n. 9, 151, 153 n. 18, 163 n. 31
compassion, 47, 94
Complementary Norms, 31 n. 15, 54 n. 46
composition of place, 43, 83, 150
confidence, 48, 132, 151, 162–163
confirmation, 15, 18, 21, 38, 41, 44, 60, 75, 85–86, 114, 130
conscience, 27 n. 9, 45, 73, 102, 130, 135, 164; *see also* account of conscience
consolation, 7–9, 60, 79, 86, 94, 118, 130, 134–135, 164
Constitutions, ix–x, 1, 3 n. 10, 4 n. 11, 5, 13–14, 17–23, 26, 29–30, 31 n. 15, 37, 41–43, 55,
     57–58, 61–67, 69–71, 75–76, 82, 89–92, 103, 109, 114, 119–120, 123, 126–127, 132, 133
     n. 20, 135, 136 nn. 25 and 26, 137, 141–142, 145–149, 154, 157, 159
          Preamble, 71, 104, 141–142, 144, 148–150
          part I, 29
          part III, 42, 44–45, 56, 63, 65–66, 71, 75, 117, 132, 144, 163 n. 31
          part IV, 78
          part V, 53
          part VI, 57, 62–65, 68, 73, 111
          part VII, 22, 31 n. 16, 55 n. 2, 63, 82–83, 86, 89–90, 92–95, 97–99, 102, 104, 147, 160
          part VIII, 17 n. 38, 22, 63, 89, 103–104, 107–118, 138, 142, 147, 149
          part IX, 113, 123, 136–137, 142, 143 n. 36, 147
          part X, 65, 110, 137, 144, 146–152, 157, 163
Contemplation to Attain Love, 34, 77, 88 n. 16, 115, 138, 148–150, 159
contemplation, 8, 45, 47, 50, 60, 75, 77, 83, 115
contemplative, 2, 10, 39, 48, 62, 97, 120, 136, 150 n. 11
continuity, 21, 150
conversation, x, 4, 8–10, 16
conversion, 4, 7, 11, 33, 37, 39, 57, 60–61, 82, 165
corporate, 1, 13, 14 n. 36, 15–16, 22–23, 63, 86, 89, 104, 112, 121, 123, 129, 134 n. 22, 135,
     138 n. 30, 144–146, 148, 159, 163
correspondence, 91, 118; *see also* letters
credibility, 26, 31 n. 17, 66, 101, 114, 153
cross, 12, 58
culture, 70, 98 n. 32, 117, 122, 127, 136, 151, 161

de arriba, 40, 115, 138
decisions, 7–8, 16, 18–19, 21, 32, 41, 47, 55 n. 2, 96, 99, 125–126, 129–130, 140, 153–154,
     156, 157 n. 23
declarations, 23 n. 56, 30, 90–92, 110, 112 n. 17, 144
Deliberation of the First Fathers, 15–19, 21, 36, 65, 89–90, 107, 125–127, 151
Desert Fathers, 7, 24, 64, 132, 133 n. 20
desire, 7, 9–10, 15, 18, 32–34, 36–37, 39–41, 49, 58, 60, 67–68, 70, 82, 89, 96–99, 130–132,
     151, 155 n. 20, 162
desolation, 118, 130
determination, 32–35, 37–41, 49, 61
developmental, 28, 56, 71, 89, 147

devoción, 45, 75, 79–80
devotion, 45–46, 52, 75–76, 79–80, 99, 132, 159
dialogue, 28, 96, 129
discernment, 6, 11, 15, 17–18, 24, 27–29, 32–33, 41, 44, 45 n. 34, 51, 55 n. 2, 61, 68, 73, 92, 94–96, 102, 113, 126, 129, 131, 135, 139, 141, 154, 156, 161
discontinuity, 24, 121 n. 38, 157
discretio, 131
dismissal, 112
dispersal, 15–16, 19, 21, 89–92, 103–104, 106–108, 118, 120, 125, 147–148
distribution, 14, 71, 93, 104, 149
doctrine, 27, 50, 93, 116–117, 124, 139
Dominic, St, 6, 9, 64, 82
dying, 10, 33, 44, 47
dynamics, 8–9, 27–29, 31–32, 43, 45, 52, 112, 116, 137, 146–149

ecclesial, 81
efficacy, 16, 36, 116, 126
election, 29, 38, 41, 45, 55, 82, 95, 129
end (of the Society), 112, 145, 161
enemy, 65–66, 101, 116–117, 131; *see also* adversaries
evangelical counsels, 32 n. 19; *see also* celibacy, chastity, obedience, poverty
evangelizing, 9, 14, 37, 61, 64–65, 101, 108, 150
evil, 49, 69
examen of conscience, 135, 150
Examen, General, 19, 26–35, 37–42, 44–46, 48–53, 63, 66–68, 75, 89, 94, 133, 145, 159–160
example, 39, 49, 69, 77, 131, 151
experience, 1, 3, 5–6, 8–9, 11–13, 16, 18, 20–22, 28, 30, 31 n. 32, 35–37, 40, 42–45, 47 n. 38, 48, 50–55, 59, 61–62, 65, 68–69, 77, 80, 85–87, 91, 93 n. 25, 96, 116, 119, 121, 123, 128–129, 139, 141 n. 32, 148, 151–152, 154, 162 n. 30
experiments, 42–54, 72, 75–76

faith, 6, 48, 77, 80, 93, 96, 123, 150, 153–156
Favre, Pierre, 12, 14, 70 n. 23, 87, 127 n. 9
fear, 48, 71
Flos sanctorum, 9
formation, 21, 27 n. 10, 42, 49 n. 40, 52–53, 62–63, 68, 73–74, 163 n. 31
Formula of the Institute, 5, 18, 21, 26–27, 58, 65, 93–94, 97, 99
Foscarari, Egidio, 132, 133 n. 19
Fourth Vow (of obedience to the Pope), 24, 31, 84, 90, 91 n. 21, 95, 104, 124 n. 5
Francis of Assisi, St, x, 6, 9, 64, 82
freedom, 14 n. 35, 30–31, 34, 39–40, 44, 60–61, 66, 74, 81, 96, 99, 111, 117, 139, 148
friendship, 11, 13–16, 30 n. 14, 34, 101 n. 38, 104, 121, 125–126, 163
fruit, 8, 46, 82, 93, 99, 101–102, 104, 161
future, 7, 22, 48, 101, 125, 144, 149–151, 154, 156, 158, 163

Ganss, George E., 110, 112, 144 n. 1, 146
General Congregation, 23 n. 56, 25 n. 3, 31 n. 16, 36 n. 24, 92 n. 24, 109, 119–121, 130
generosity, 10, 34, 49, 60, 69, 102, 112, 151
gifts, 43, 115, 138, 152, 157; *see also* gratuity
glory, 8–11, 14, 38, 40, 53, 66, 72, 82, 90, 93–94, 97, 99, 104, 107, 129, 142, 144, 149, 159, 162
God, ix, 5–9, 12, 15, 17, 20, 22, 28, 30, 32–34, 44, 46, 48–49, 52–53, 56, 58, 60, 62–64, 66, 70–72, 75–79, 82, 87, 90, 93–99, 104, 108, 114–118, 126, 128–130, 135, 138–139, 141–143, 145–146, 148–151, 153–156, 158–163; *see also* Trinity
gospel, 21, 65, 85, 101, 112 n. 18, 133 n. 19
Gouveia, Diego de, 14

governance, 22, 89, 95, 104, 107, 114, 118, 123–126, 129–130, 132–133, 135, 137, 141–143, 146–147, 149
grace, 8, 12, 20, 40, 43–45, 49, 53, 62, 65, 67, 72, 74–75, 79–81, 87, 128–130, 135, 138, 143 n. 34, 145, 149–150, 154, 158, 160, 162–163
grades, 27
gratitude, 99, 148
gratuity, 115
growth, 23, 50, 65, 71, 89, 98 n. 32, 111 n. 15, 131, 133, 145, 148, 150, 158, 160, 162, 163 n. 31

head (of the body), 22, 100, 103, 113, 124 n. 6, 127, 138, 142
heart, 53, 59, 63, 69, 89, 109, 112–113, 116, 127, 137, 146–147, 151
Hernández, Bartolomé, 79
hierarchy, 100, 113, 143, 151 n. 12
Holy Spirit, 85–86, 96, 107, 113, 136
honour, 40, 47, 67, 149
hospital, 42, 46–50, 94
hospitality, 122
house, 29–30, 31 n. 15, 42, 49–50, 56, 68, 84, 93, 99, 103, 105–107, 112, 120, 151
humility, 20, 50, 52–53, 84, 98, 111, 116, 135, 137–138

Ignatius of Loyola, St, 28, 30, 50–51, 59–62, 70, 74–79, 105–107, 127–128, 131–133, 140–141, 143, 149, 158
    as founder of the Jesuits, ix–x, 16–21, 25, 33–39, 41–42, 46–48, 56, 63, 67–68, 74–79, 90–93, 95, 97–101, 108–114, 117–118, 123–125, 128, 135–137, 151, 161–163
    life of, 1–13, 38–39, 41–42, 46–47, 57–58, 60, 64–65, 79, 86–87, 95, 100, 152–156
    as mystic, 1–2, 8–9, 85–87, 152–157
imagination, 43, 77, 82–83, 96, 106, 121, 152–153
incarnation, 22, 55, 62, 86, 87 n. 15, 89, 96, 105
indifference, 27–28, 43–44, 81, 91, 95, 110
individual, 9, 16, 22–23, 31, 44, 50, 56, 63, 70–71, 82 n. 2, 96, 112, 117, 120, 131–132, 134–135, 138 n. 30, 142, 144, 146 n. 6, 149, 151, 163
institute, 7, 21, 25, 29, 55–56, 63, 65–66, 68, 73, 116, 119, 125, 146 n. 6, 154
instrumentality, 56, 78, 159–162
instruments, 96, 146, 159–162
intellect, 53, 77, 86, 152, 155
intention, 30, 35, 59, 63, 70–72, 78, 80, 90, 95, 159

Jaer, André de, 55, 57
Jerusalem, 11, 60–61, 64, 106–107
Jesuits; *see* Society of Jesus
Jesus, 12, 39, 54–55, 58, 60, 62, 65, 68, 76, 82–88, 97, 106–108, 114–115, 124, 159; *see also* Christ
John III (of Portugal), 100
journeys, 12–13, 49 n. 40, 53, 57 n. 4, 61, 82–84, 87, 90, 106–107
judgment, 14, 63, 88, 99, 110, 116–117, 132, 139–140
justice, 98 n. 32, 122

kenosis, 47
Kingdom, 65, 67, 83, 98, 106, 127, 137 n. 27
knowledge, 28, 32, 42 n. 30, 53, 133–134, 155

La Storta, 12, 87, 154
labour, 7, 10, 77–79, 84, 93, 98, 111, 134, 145, 158–159
Laínez, Diego, 5, 12, 51, 57, 58 n. 5, 87, 100 n. 36, 114 n. 21
law, 127
letters, 14, 35 n. 23, 63–64, 68–69, 76–79, 91, 97–98, 116, 118–119; *see also* correspondence
liberty; *see* freedom

love, 22, 34, 39, 48, 53, 59, 66–67, 69, 71–72, 78, 81, 88, 96, 108, 114–116, 121, 132, 138, 140, 149
Loyola, 7, 9, 57, 58 n. 59, 60, 82, 154

magis, 97, 99, 148
magnanimity, 34, 139
manifestation (of conscience), 102, 130, 135; *see also* account of conscience
Manresa, 7–9, 20–21, 39, 57, 64, 86–87, 152, 155
Mass, 12, 55 n. 1, 158 n. 24
means (and ends), 10, 15, 37, 39, 63, 99, 108–109, 117, 135, 146, 151, 158–163
meditation, 12, 45, 72–73, 76–77, 83, 151
members, 6–7, 16, 22–23, 28, 43, 55, 58, 65–66, 71, 86, 89, 92–93, 97, 100, 102–105, 108, 93 n. 25, 109, 111, 113, 115, 117, 122, 125, 127–130, 132, 134 n. 22, 136, 142, 144–145, 147–149, 152, 160, 163; *see also* subjects
mendicancy, 4, 24, 48, 64, 68, 105; *see also* begging
metaphor, 65–66, 74, 101, 107, 125, 127–128, 159–161
ministry, 7, 12–15, 26, 31 n. 17, 35, 37, 41–42, 44, 46–47, 49 n. 40, 50–52, 59–60, 66, 68 n. 18, 81, 84–86, 90, 92, 94–95, 99–100, 103, 105–106, 128, 140, 145, 161, 163 n. 31
Miró, Diego, 92 n. 23, 100
mission, 13, 15–17, 22, 24, 31, 34–35, 38–39, 55–56, 58, 61 n. 10, 63–64, 66, 68, 70, 81–83, 85–93, 95–96, 98, 102–107, 112, 115, 117 n. 26, 119–122, 125–126, 129–130, 132–136, 138 n. 30, 142, 145–148, 163
mobility, 91, 103, 157
moderation, 35 n. 23, 74, 147 n. 8
mortification, 39, 70, 72, 110–111; 132
movements, 8, 58 n. 5, 91, 115
multiplying (effect), 100–102, 118, 129
mystic, 2, 8–9, 35, 48, 62, 69, 85–87, 111, 115, 152, 154, 157
mystical, 69, 93 n. 25, 115 n. 24, 156 n. 21

Nadal, Jerónimo, x, 4–6, 12 n. 29, 14 n. 32, 20, 26, 33, 46, 52, 71, 83–85, 92, 98, 105–106, 145, 154, 156
natural, 47, 96, 111, 156 n. 21, 160, 162–163
need, 14–15, 92, 97–99, 134
novices, 31 nn. 13 and 15, 41–42, 44–54, 56, 65, 71–72, 75, 132
novitiate, 21, 29–30, 32–34, 41–42, 45, 49, 51–53, 56–57, 75

obedience, 17–18, 21, 24, 26 n. 6, 31, 35 n. 23, 47, 49, 55–56, 58, 61–64, 73, 75, 78, 91, 93 n. 25, 104, 111–113, 126, 130, 143
obligations, 125
Onfroy, François, 35 n. 23, 74–75
Onuphrius, 7–8
ordination (priestly), 12, 17 n. 39, 27, 65, 79 n. 32
orthodoxy, 139

Oviedo, Andrea de, 35 n. 23, 74
Paris, 3 n. 10, 4 n. 11, 6, 11, 13, 42, 58, 64, 79, 125
Paul III (Pope), 18, 51, 95 nn. 27 and 28
peace, 10, 44
penances, 7, 24, 47 n. 38, 73–74, 132
perfection, 39–40, 43, 63, 65, 137, 140, 145, 162 n. 29
personal, 1, 9, 22, 32–33, 38, 40, 56, 67 n. 17, 70, 78, 87, 94, 112–113, 121, 133–135, 138 n. 30, 139, 159, 162, 163 n. 31
pilgrimage, 7, 9, 42, 48, 49 n. 40, 61–62, 64, 82 n. 4, 106–107
Polanco, Juan de, ix, 3, 7, 11 n. 27, 19–20, 35 n. 23, 42, 68–69, 74, 92 n. 23, 115, 118, 124, 136
polarities, 16–17, 137, 157–158, 163

poor, 40–41, 47, 49, 59, 65, 67–69, 121
Pope, 13–15, 18, 24, 31, 90, 95, 104, 125–126
portrait, 1, 136–137, 141
possessions, 34
poverty, 14 n. 35, 17 n. 39, 20, 26 n. 6, 38 n. 27, 40, 48, 52, 55–56, 58, 61 n. 11–62, 64–69, 85, 124, 137, 147 n. 8
praise, 3, 28, 40, 138 n. 30, 149–150, 158
prayer, 5, 10–12, 20, 30, 32, 34–35, 50, 56, 60, 69–77, 79, 81–82, 96, 101 n. 38, 129–130, 138, 148, 151, 158, 162 n. 30
preaching, 37, 42, 51, 64, 83–85, 93, 106, 124, 160
presupposition, 41, 43, 56, 73, 82, 95, 112, 123–124, 127, 129–130, 141–142
priesthood, 13, 27, 35–37, 42, 58, 90, 94, 126
priests, 12, 14, 27, 35–36, 50–51, 98, 111 n. 16, 126
priority, 17, 103, 105
probation, 12 n. 28, 29–30, 31 n. 15, 52–53, 71–72, 84, 132, 144
professed, 53, 55–56, 63, 65, 68, 71, 73–76, 84, 91, 99, 110, 119–120, 124, 134
progress, 23, 30 n. 14, 53, 56, 71–72, 93, 99, 144–145, 149
project, 5, 81, 118, 124, 144
providence, 52, 96, 123, 141–143, 150–151, 160–163
psychology, 3, 69–70, 76, 118, 120
purity, 57, 58 n. 59–60, 62–63, 70, 72, 78, 80

reconciliation, 94
Reformation, 14
Reformers, 13, 14 n. 36, 24, 101
Regimini militantis ecclesiae, 18
religious, 7, 17, 24–25, 26 n. 6, 28, 31–33, 35–38, 40–41, 57–58, 62–63, 65, 68 n. 19, 69, 72, 94 n. 26, 108, 123, 130, 145 n. 4, 163 n. 31
renunciation, 38–39, 41
repetition, 50, 53
reputation, 140, 162
résumé, 146–147
revenue, 68
reverence, 39, 67, 77, 157
Ribadeneira, Pedro de, 110, 136 n. 26
riches, 38 n. 27
road, 46, 49, 83, 106
Rodrigues, Simão, ix, 47, 111
Rules for Discernment, 131, 161
rules, 29, 42, 58 n. 6, 120, 136 n. 26

Salmerón, Alfonso, 51
scholastics, 27, 35 n. 23, 53, 56, 71–72, 75–79, 110
secularity, 24, 25 n. 3, 77, 80, 122, 140, 149, 155–157, 163
sending, 15, 81–83, 85–86, 89, 91–97, 101–102, 107, 129, 134
sentir, 87
sexuality, 59–62
Siete Partidas, 127, 137 n. 27; *see also* law
sin, 3, 42, 68
Society of Jesus, 24, 26, 35–38, 41, 43, 46 n. 35, 48–53, 58, 61, 68–71, 74, 84–85, 90, 92, 94–96, 99, 101, 106–107, 115–116, 118, 127–130, 139–143, 153–154, 160
   as a body, 21–23, 26–27, 31, 33–34, 40, 55–56, 62–64, 86, 88–89, 93, 100, 103–105, 109–114, 119–128, 133–135, 138, 144–152, 158–159, 162–163
   foundation of, ix–x, 6, 14, 17–20, 25, 29, 91, 157–158
   and the Pope; *see* Fourth Vow

souls, 8–9, 11, 43, 46 n. 35, 55, 72, 74, 82, 84, 93, 104, 106, 134, 138, 145, 150, 158–159, 161
spirit, 4, 22–23, 25–26, 44, 53, 59, 69, 70 n. 23, 73, 75, 85–86, 89, 94, 107–108, 113, 130, 135–136, 139, 151, 156, 158, 161
Spiritual Diary, 7, 20, 68–69, 86, 124
spiritual direction, 32, 133 nn. 20 and 21
Spiritual Exercises, 1 n. 1, 2–3, 11, 15, 18, 29–30, 40–42, 45, 50, 52, 54, 64, 66, 70, 81, 91 n. 21, 94–95, 99, 108 n. 10, 115 n. 24, 128–129, 131, 139–140, 143 n. 36, 146 n. 6, 148–149
spirituality, x, 1, 7–9, 11, 16, 24 n. 2, 58, 76 n. 29, 82 n. 2, 86, 87 n. 15, 115 n. 24, 118, 145 n. 4, 152 n. 15, 163,
states (of life), 71
studies, 11, 27, 53, 56, 64, 71–72, 75–79
subjects, 22, 95, 109–110, 113–115, 133–134, 141; *see also* members, 23 n. 56
subsidiarity, 113
Superior General, 95, 123–124, 127
        authority, 18, 91, 95, 100–101, 143 n. 36
        election, 19
        qualities, 1, 113–114, 125 n. 7, 137–142
superiors, 22, 23 n. 56, 29–30, 51, 56, 62, 73–74, 93, 95–96, 102, 106, 109, 113, 115, 123–125, 129–130, 132–136, 141–143, 147 n. 8, 158
supernatural, 25 n. 3, 162

talents, 111, 134, 139, 157
temptations, 3, 130, 132
tension, 16–17, 106–107, 157 n. 23
tertians, 12 n. 28, 52–54
testament, 4
Trinity, 7–8, 10, 85–87, 96–97, 115, 148, 152, 154–155
Two Standards, 12, 67–68, 83, 116, 124, 161

uniformity, 116–118
union, 16–17, 21–22, 39, 63, 89, 91 n. 22, 103–104, 106, 108–114, 116–118, 126, 128, 130, 145–147, 157, 161–162
unitive, 62–63, 82, 111–112, 162 n. 30
universal, 10, 41, 90–91, 95, 97, 100, 105, 112, 116, 119–120, 144

Vatican II, 98 n. 32, 120, 130
virtue, 4, 56, 59, 62, 70, 72, 111, 116, 132, 138–140, 150, 159
vocation, 15, 24, 30, 35–36, 41, 43, 56, 85, 90, 98, 131, 151
vows, 34, 55–58

way of proceeding, 7, 11, 27 n. 10, 58, 64, 95, 163
Week (of the Exercises), 38, 53–54, 67 n. 17, 82, 84, 116, 131, 148–149
will, 10, 14–15, 17–18, 34, 44, 53, 60, 63, 87–88, 135, 138 n. 30, 151
wisdom, 96, 131, 141, 150, 152, 156
word, 51–52, 67, 86, 87 n. 15, 94, 107, 156, 160
work, 3, 26, 47, 51, 53, 62, 72, 78, 81, 84, 88, 93, 98, 111, 145, 158, 161
world, 10, 13, 15, 32, 34–35, 37, 38 n. 27, 40, 46, 54, 67, 72, 81–82, 84, 86, 90–91, 93, 104–105, 107, 121–122, 124, 128, 134, 145, 150, 155, 159, 161

Xavier, St Francis, 54, 116

zeal, 4, 159